TENNIS:
BACK TO THE BASICS
THIRD EDITION

by

Carole J. Zebas, P.E.D.
University of Kansas
Lawrence, Kansas

and

H. Mardi Johnson, M.S.
Tennis Professional
Phoenix, Arizona

eddie bowers publishing, inc.
2600 Jackson Street
Dubuque, Iowa 52001

LIBRARY
ST. LOUIS COMMUNITY COLLEGE
AT FLORISSANT VALLEY

ACKNOWLEDGEMENTS

The authors would like to acknowledge a number of people who assisted in the completion of this book. Thanks to Dan Davis, Karen Elquest, Don Gillett, Mario Hill, Molly Murphy, John Muczko, Robert Ofstedahl, and Erin Reid for posing as the subjects in the photograph. A special thanks to our photographer Robert Ofstedahl and to the Arizona Sports Ranch and Gold Key Racquet Club for the photo background. The graphics were done by Yvonne Joseph and Russell Hailey. Finally, a thank you to Steve Yeager for the new chapter inspiration and to Dr. Nancy King for writing the chapter.

eddie bowers publishing, inc.
2600 Jackson Street
Dubuque, Iowa 52001-3342

ISBN 0-945483-66-X

Copyright © 1997, by *eddie bowers publishing, inc.*

All rights reserved. No part of this publication may be reproduced, stored in a retrieval system, or transmitted, in any form or by any means, electronic, mechanical, photocopy, recording or otherwise, without the prior written permission of *eddie bowers publishing, inc.*

Printed in the United States of America.

9 8 7 6 5 4 3 2 1

TABLE OF CONTENTS

PREFACE

With the many excellent tennis books out on the market today, one wonders why another text needs to be written. The answer is simple. The authors feel that what they have to offer to teaching and learning the fundamentals of tennis is the combined expertise of a teaching professional in tennis who has experienced working with all age groups and skill levels, and a biomechanist who has taught the analysis of tennis skills by drawing on concepts of physics. The unique combination of theory and practice provides a complete approach to the game. Having both been students and teachers of the game they are sensitive to the potential problems other learners and teachers face.

Tennis can be broken down into several very basic and fundamental movements. The authors believe that too much information can become confusing, thus concentration on the task at hand becomes difficult. Further, the authors strongly feel that a positive approach should be taken in the learning or

teaching of tennis skills. This book was written with the tennis *player* and the tennis *teacher* in mind. It is a known fact that when professional tennis players fall into a "slump" they resort back to the basic fundamental mechanics of each stroke. They start from the beginning as they search for clues in solving the mystery of their slump. Each phase of each stroke is broken down into its parts because they know that all skills need to built upon a sound base.

The objective of this book, therefore, is to provide the information necessary to develop a mechanically sound tennis stroke. In keeping with the "back to the basics" approach, key fundamental points in the development of the stroke are highlighted in the "Checklist" section. Photographs have been included to emphasize important phases of the skill.

A unique feature of this book is the "Analysis of Tennis Strokes" chapter. This chapter is designed to assist the player in self analysis or the teacher in the systematic observation of the mechanics of each of the four basic strokes. The authors have attempted to "key" in on the movement patterns which are most likely to be altered in an unsuccessful stroking motion. Teaching cues are provided to detect and correct the errors in movement.

Several other features make this book valuable for both the player and the teacher of tennis. Special practice drills for individuals and groups are provided. Strategy for game situations are included for both singles and doubles play. Descriptions on equipment and facilities are based on the latest scientific information. A conditioning chapter has been included to optimize physical development to enhance the strength, speed, balance, and endurance required for tennis. A chapter on the use of visualization for the improvement of skill performance has been included. Finally, there is information concerning the USTA as a resource for educational and recreational materials, a set of condensed official rules, a set of unwritten rules, a glossary of common tennis terminology, and a sample written tennis examination.

TENNIS: Then and Now

Then

Now

It is speculated that the ancient version of tennis had its beginnings in China over 5000 years ago. Players were observed hitting a ball back and forth with an implement resembling a racquet. More substantial evidence of a game resembling tennis was found in France during the 14th century. A game known as "jeu de courte paume" (played indoors) and "jeu de longue tennis" (played outdoors) was enjoyed by the upper middle classes. The game essentially involved hitting a ball with the bare hands over a rope. The ball was stuffed with animal hair or cloth and covered with sheepskin. Later gloves, which originally were used to protect the hands, were replaced with "battoirs" or wooden clubs. The forerunner of the racquet we know today was developed in the 15th century. It probably was about this time that the term tennis also was coined. It was derived from the French word "tenez" which means "to take" or "to play".

The modern game of tennis had its beginnings in 1873 when Major Walter Clopton Wingfield introduced a game to the British upper echelon which he called "Sphairistike", a Greek word meaning "to play". It was played on an hour-glass shape grass court, and scored much like a badminton game. The name "Sphairistike" later became known as "tennis-on-the-lawn", and then again was shortened to a simpler name, "lawn tennis".

About the time that lawn tennis was becoming popular, the All-England Croquet Club was experiencing some difficult financial times. They decided to host a lawn tennis championship for fund-raising purposes. So in 1877, the first Wimbledon Championships were held. This is now considered to be the most prestigious of all tennis championships.

The game of tennis was introduced in the United States around 1875. Mary Outerbridge, a New Yorker visiting in Bermuda, became interested in the game while she was on vacation. She learned to play the game, and when she returned home she brought with her skills and equipment. It took several years for the game to "catch on" in the United States, but by 1881 the first National Lawn Tennis Tournament was played.

One other important development occurred in 1881. Several variations of the game were being played with all different rules. A brother of Mary Outerbridge was responsible for convening a meeting of tennis club officials in the New York area for the purpose of establishing a standardized set of rules. Thus was born the United States Lawn Tennis Association (USLTA). This organization would later become known as the United States Tennis Association (USTA) when surfaces other than grass became popular to play on. The U.S. National Championships, one of the four major competitions, was first held in the same year. The French Open and Australian Open later would be added to complete the "big four" in tennis championships,   referred to now as the Grand Slam.

In 1909, Davis Cup competition between men's teams from the United States and England popularized the sport even more. (This later was expanded to include teams from all nations.) Women, who began competition with Wimbledon in 1884, had the Wightman Cup competition. This brought together teams from the United States and England   in 1923. The Federation Cup competition for women of all nations was organized in 1963.

Whereas in the early days of tennis when only the upper class played the sport, today people of all walks of life play the game. Tennis playing facilities are available for virtually anyone who desires to learn the game. There are private and public facilities to accommodate all economic classes, and there are indoor and outdoor facilities for all-weather conditions.

Perhaps the greatest popularity growth in tennis occurred in the late 1960's. The sport became a lucrative one when big money prizes were being offered to professional players. It also was the time when open tennis became popular by allowing professionals and amateurs to compete with one another. Amateurs could compete and still retain their amateur standing while professionals could compete in the prestigious tournaments for prize money.

The lure of the big money prizes and television exposure brought thousands of would-be stars to the courts. Not all would or could become professionals. Interestingly enough, many of those who would not go on to play professionally still maintained a high interest in playing the game. It was an activity to keep physically fit, it permitted one to socialize with friends, it provided an outlet for those who craved competition, it was a year-around activity, and it could be played by people of all ages.

Today, tennis remains a popular "lifetime" sport. Once the game has been learned, there are ample opportunities for tournament competition. For those who have membership in a private or public club, tournaments based on age and skill levels, are conducted regularly. Most community owned courts also provide opportunities for competition. These, too, are based on age groups and/or skill levels.

One way competition can be equalized is by classifying individuals according to skill level. The USTA has a rating scale which attempts to classify individuals with similar skills. The general rating categories are:

National Tennis Rating Program	
Beginner	1.6 - 2.5
Advanced Beginner	2.6 - 3.5
Intermediate	3.6 - 4.5
Advanced	4.6 - 5.5

Whether competing for money or playing for enjoyment and personal challenge is your goal, tennis is a game which can continue to be a gratifying experience throughout a lifetime. Developing the appropriate skills will enhance your enjoyment of the game. Classes are offered through recreation departments, university/college physical education departments, and clubs. Private lessons and clinics are offered by teaching professionals.

Chapter 2

CONDITIONING & WARMING UP:
Getting in Shape to Play

Tennis is a game of starts, stops, and changes of direction. In order to perform with maximum efficiency and with the least threat of injury, the body must be in condition. When you become fatigued, the feet "feel" very heavy. The body fails to respond quickly to the ball, and the strokes become more difficult to execute. The lack of proper footwork causes the timing of the stroke to be disrupted. It further has been demonstrated that a body which lacks strength or flexibility is more susceptible to injury. Thus, it would seem logical to follow a conditioning program which would alleviate these problems and make the game of tennis more enjoyable.

Conditioning programs generally consist of three parts: strength and power development, stretching/flexibility, and cardio-vascular endurance/aerobics. Each program will be discussed with illustrations of recommended exercises offered. The muscles being strengthened or stretched may be found on the accompanying muscle charts (Figures 2.1 and 2.2).

STRENGTH AND POWER DEVELOPMENT

Why do you need to have strength and power to play the game of tennis? The answer is simple. You need them for body control, racquet control, coordination, quickness, and explosiveness. Most recreational or weekend players do not give serious consideration to a strength and power development program because they cannot see the benefits which may accrue. Secondly, these players usually do not have access to a weight facility, or simply do not know how to get started. It is no wonder that strength and power programs have not been popular for tennis players. It only has been recently that even the professionals have begun to see the benefits of such programs.

The terms strength and power have been used here, and should be defined. Strength may be thought of as a force that a muscle exerts against a resistance in one maximal effort. Power

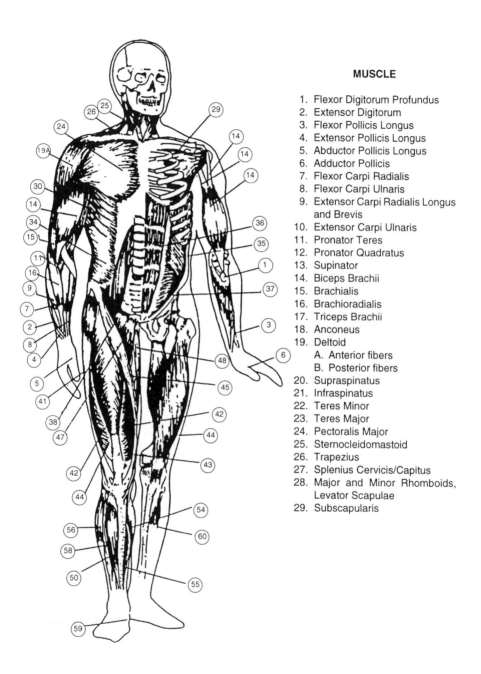

MUSCLE

1. Flexor Digitorum Profundus
2. Extensor Digitorum
3. Flexor Pollicis Longus
4. Extensor Pollicis Longus
5. Abductor Pollicis Longus
6. Adductor Pollicis
7. Flexor Carpi Radialis
8. Flexor Carpi Ulnaris
9. Extensor Carpi Radialis Longus and Brevis
10. Extensor Carpi Ulnaris
11. Pronator Teres
12. Pronator Quadratus
13. Supinator
14. Biceps Brachii
15. Brachialis
16. Brachioradialis
17. Triceps Brachii
18. Anconeus
19. Deltoid
    A. Anterior fibers
    B. Posterior fibers
20. Supraspinatus
21. Infraspinatus
22. Teres Minor
23. Teres Major
24. Pectoralis Major
25. Sternocleidomastoid
26. Trapezius
27. Splenius Cervicis/Capitus
28. Major and Minor Rhomboids, Levator Scapulae
29. Subscapularis

Figure 2.1 *Anterior view of muscular system. Reproduced with permission of Cramer Products, Inc., Gardner, KS.*

30. Serratus Anterior
31. Erector Spinae
32. Latissimus Dorsi
33. Quadratus Lumborum
34. External Abdominal Oblique
35. Internal Abdominal Oblique
36. Rectus Abdominus
37. Transversus Abdominus
38. Iliopsoas Pectineus
39. Gluteus Medius
40. Gluteus Maximum
41. Tensor Fasciae Latae
42. Rectus Femoris
43. Vastus Medialis
44. Vastus Lateralis
45. Sartorius
46. Adductor Magnus
47. Adductor Longus
48. Gracilia
49. Biceps Femoris
50. Semimembranosus
51. Semitendinosus
52. Popliteus
53. Plantaris
54. Gastrocnemius
55. Soleus
56. Peroneus Longus
57. Peroneus Brevis
58. Extensor Digitorum Longus
59. Extensor Hallicus Longus
60. Tibialis Anterior
61. Tibialis Posterior
62. Flexor Digitorum Longus
63. Flexor Hallicus Longus

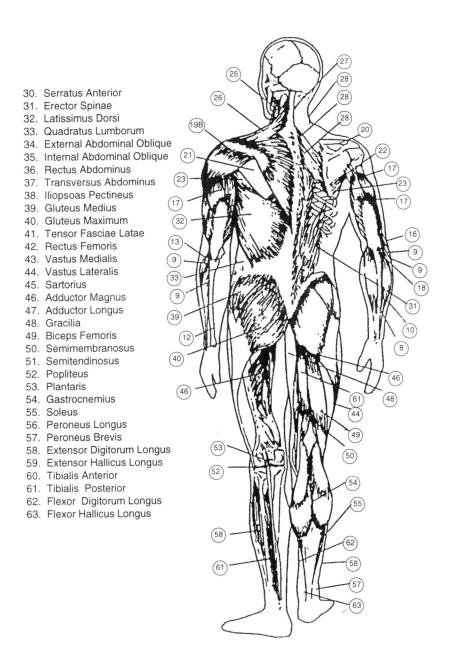

Figure 2.2 *Posterior view of muscular system. Reproduced with permission of Cramer Products, Inc., Gardner, KS.*

is exerting a force with a time consideration, or how much work can be performed per unit of time. Strength can best be gained by working with heavier weights and fewer repetitions. Power is best developed by using lighter weights and more repetitions. Both involve the principle of overload. That is, in order for a training effect to occur the muscles must work harder than usual in moving a resistance.

Two popular pieces of equipment which are available for providing the necessary resistance to develop strength and power are free weights and machines such as Universal, Nautilus, or Hydra-Fitness. A few words of caution should be made before a strengh/power program is begun. Consult with a qualified strength and conditioning expert before attempting any lifts. They will show you how to use the equipment properly and how to perform the activity correctly. If you are over 35 years of age, you should consult with your physician before beginning a new program.

Remember that building bulky muscles is not the objective of a strength/power program for tennis players. Tennis players need muscular development which allows them to move quickly around the court. For that reason, it is suggested that a "power" oriented conditioning program be used. This means that lighter weights should be used with more repetitions. Some general guidelines for lifting weights are:

1. Lift lighter weights with at least 10 to 15 rapid repetitions. If you cannot perform the movement for at least 10 repetitions, the weight you are using is too heavy.
2. Alternate opposing muscle groups (e.g. quadriceps and hamstrings).
3. Repeat a set of 10 to 15 repetitions for 2 or 3 times. You can, for instance, do a set of 10 to 15 repetitions for the quadriceps, then do the same for the hamstrings. Repeat the entire sequence for a second time.
4. Move the weights through a full range of motion.
5. Continue breathing throughout the exercise.
6. Use explosive movements when exercising in the opposite direction as the force of gravity (concentric contraction).
7. Use slower movements when exercising in the same direction as the force of gravity (eccentric contraction).

Table 2.1 can be used to find the muscles and exercises most involved in the basic tennis strokes.

Table 2.1. *Basic Strokes, Muscles Used, and Exercises*

Stroke	Muscles	Strength Exercise	Stretching Exercise
Forehand	Hamstrings	2.16	2.20
	Quadriceps	2.15	2.21
	Gastroc/Soleus	2.17	2.23
	Pectorals	2.3, 2.4, 2.5	2.26
	Latissimus dorsi	2.5, 2.8	2.18, 2.22
	Deltoids	2.3, 2.4, 2.6, 2.7	2.26
	Biceps	2.5, 2.9	2.26
	Extensor, Flexor Carpi Radialis	2.12	
	Abdominals	2.13 a & b	2.19
	Erector Spinae	2.14	2.18, 2.22
	Gluteals	2.14	2.18, 2.22
Backhand	Hamstrings	2.16	2.20
	Quadriceps	2.15	2.21
	Gastroc/Soleus	2.17	2.23
	Trapezius	2.7	
	Rhomboids	2.5, 2.7,	
	Extensor, Flexor Carpi Radialis	2.12	2.28
	Abdominals	2.13	2.19
	Erector Spinae	2.14	2.18, 2.22
	Gluteals	2.14	2.18, 2.22
Volley	Hamstrings	2.16	2.20
	Quadriceps	2.15	2.21
	Gastroc/Soleus	2.17	2.23
	Extensor, Flexor Carpi Radialis	2.12	2.28
	Abdominals	2.13 a & b	2.19
	Erector Spinae	2.14	2.18, 2.22
	Gluteals	2.14	2.18, 2.22
Serve	Hamstrings	2.16	2.20
	Quadriceps	2.15	2.21
	Gastroc/Soleus	2.17	2.23
	Abdominals	2.13 a & b	2.19
	Erector Spinae	2.14	2.18, 2.22
	Gluteals	2.14	2.18, 2.22
	Triceps	2.3, 2.4, 2.10	2.25
	Rotator Cuff	2.11	2.27
	Extensor, Flexor Carpi Radialis	2.12	
	Supinator	2.12	
	Pronators	2.12	

For further detailed information, consult a text specifically devoted to muscular training. Samples for strength/power development are provided in Figures 2.3-2.17. Refer to the muscle charts (Figure 2.1 and Figure 2.2) to locate the muscles being exercised. Notice that the program concentrates on the large muscle groups of the legs, shoulders, arms, and trunk.

Figure 2.3   *Chest press. (Pectorals, Deltoids, Triceps)*

Figure 2.4   *Push-Up. (Pectorals, Deltoids, Triceps)*

Figure 2.5   *Pull-Up.   (Biceps, Brachialis, Brachioradialis, Pectorals, Latissimus Dorsi, Rhomboids)*

Figure 2.6   *Fly. (Deltoids)*

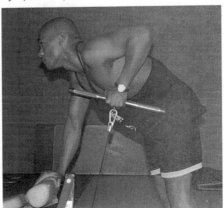

Figure 2.7   *Bench row. (Trapezius, Deltoids, Rhomboids)*

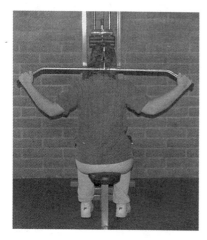

Figure 2.8   *Lat pull. (Latissimus Dorsi)*

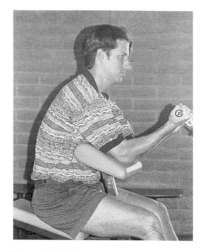

Figure 2.9   *Biceps curl. (Biceps)*

Figure 2.10   *Triceps extension. (Triceps)*

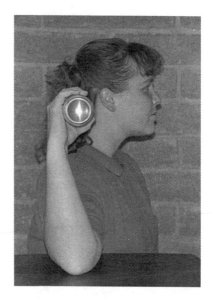

Figure 2.11   *Rotator cuff, inward-outward rotation.   (Teres Minor Subscapularis, Infraspinatus, Supraspinatus)*

Figure 2.12 *Wrist curls and rotations. (Flexor Carpi Radialis and Ulnaris, Extensor Carpi Radialis and Ulnaris, Supinators, Pronators)*

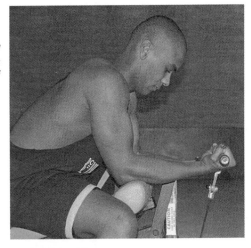

Figure 2.13a *Curl -Up. (Rectus Abdominus)*

Figure 2.13b *Curl-Up with twist. (External and Internal Obliques)*

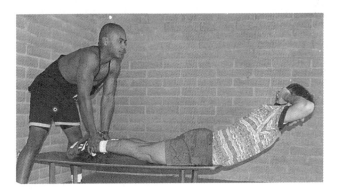

Figure 2.14 *Trunk extension. (Erector Spinae, Gluteals)*

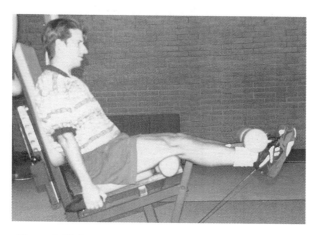

Figure 2.15 *Leg extension. (Quadriceps)*

Figure 2.16 *Leg curls.*
(Hamstrings)

Figure 2.17 *Toe raises.*
(Gastrocnemius, Soleus)

FLEXIBILITY

It is not uncommon to see participants in any sport activity stretching before the actual event. Tennis players are no different. Flexibility in the joints is needed for several reasons. It improves performance by increasing the range of motion about a joint, prevents tearing injuries to the connective tissue surrounding the muscles and joints, promotes muscle relaxation, and prevents muscle soreness.

There are several methods for stretching, but the "static" stretching method generally is the preferred method of performing the stretches. This is a slow stretch through a range of motion with a hold position at the end of the stretch. The following guidelines will be helpful in performing the stretching exercises.

1. Warm the muscles up first by light jogging or brisk walking for about 5 minutes.
2. Exercise opposing muscle groups and exercise both sides of the body.
3. Stretch slowly to the point of discomfort, but not to the point of pain.
4. Continue breathing throughout the exercise.
5. Hold each stretch from 10 to 20 seconds.
6. Repeat each exercise 2-4 times before moving on to the next exercise.
7. Stretch *before* and *after* playing.

The illustrated exercises are examples of stretching exercises which may be used (Figure 2.18-2.29). Table 2.1 can again be used to find the muscles most involved in the basic tennis strokes (see page 9). The location of the muscle(s) being stretched may be found on the muscle charts (Figures 2.1 and 2.2) on pages 6 and 7.

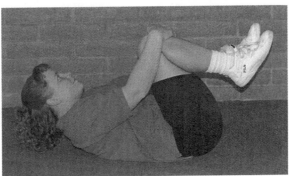

Figure 2.18 *Lower back stretch.*

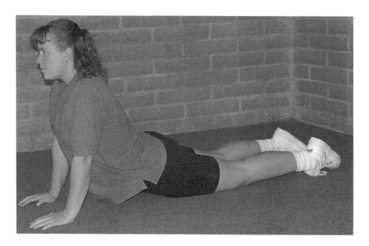

Figure 2.19 *Abdominal stretch.*

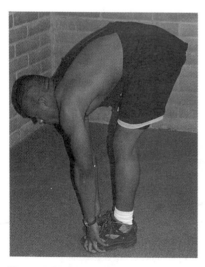

Figure 2.20 *Hamstrings stretch.*

Figure 2.21 *Quadriceps stretch.*

Figure 2.22   *Gluteal stretch.*

Figure 2.23 *Gastrocnemius/soleus stretch.*

Figure 2.24 *Anterior tibialis stretch.*

Figure 2.26 *Biceps/ pectorals stretch.*

Figure 2.25 *Triceps stretch.*

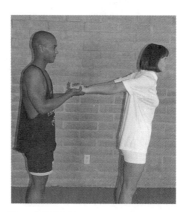

Figure 2.27 *Partner assisted rotator cuff stretch.*

Figure 2.28 *Wrist flexor/extensor stretch.*

Figure 2.29 *Ankle rotation stretch.*

CARDIOVASCULAR ENDURANCE

The game of tennis is not an aerobic exercise because it consists of stops and starts. Aerobic exercise involves a continuous pattern of movement while the heart beats faster than normal. Aerobic conditioning is needed to allow you to play several sets of tennis without becoming unduly fatigued.

Several activities provide good aerobic conditioning. They are jogging, swimming, cycling, rope jumping, brisk walking and inline skating. For improvement to occur in cardiovascular fitness, frequency of exercise, duration of exercise, and intensity of exercise must be considered. It has been suggested that aerobic exercises be done at least 3 and possibly up to 5 times per week. Each of the aerobic sessions should be 30 to 60 minutes in duration. The intensity of the exercise is based upon the heart rate. A good intensity of training would be 60% to 80% of maximal heart rate (Hrmax).

A simple and easy way to calculate the exercise target heart rate (THR) is:

HRmax	= 220 - age (years)
THR	= Hrmax x .70
Example:	
HR maximum	= 220 - 30 yrs = 190 beats/min.
THR	= 190 x 0.70 = 133 beats/min

The 133 beats per minute is the target training zone. While performing the aerobic exercise, the heart rate should remain at this level. For higher intensity training, increase the per cent of Hrmax to 75% or 80%.

WARMING UP

A well-rounded conditioning program consisting of strength/power development, flexibility development, and aerobics will be beneficial over the long term for any level of tennis player. The results will be seen in more efficient performances and reduced injury risk. However, we also should be concerned for the short-term benefits of warming up prior to practice or playing a match.

Since tennis contains power movements, large ranges of motion, and many repetitions of the same movement, it is important to include both a warmup and stretching activity before the actual practice period or match begins. Warmup may consist of light jogging or "easy" stroking of the tennis ball. After approximately five minutes or so, stretching of the important muscle groups should take place.

Chapter 3

GROUNDSTROKES:
Back to the Basics

The forehand and backhand drives are the two basic groundstrokes in tennis. These strokes generally are taught first because they allow people to "play" the game immediately. The more advanced strokes used in tennis build on the concepts found in these basic groundstrokes. Other advanced strokes which utilize some of the fundamental mechanics of the forehand and backhand drives are the approach, lob, drop shot, and return of serve. Additionally, topspin and slice sometimes are added in stroking the ball to cause changes in the direction and speed of the ball.

Most beginning tennis players assume that the forehand drive is the easiest stroke to learn, but in reality it mechanically is more difficult than the one-handed backhand. Because the hitting shoulder, arm, and racquet are farthest from the oncoming ball after the initial reaction phase, the timing is more difficult. That is, the hip, shoulder, arm and racquet must turn to and through the ball as one unit for control, power, and consistency.Softball or baseball players who have swung a bat at a ball see a likeness to the tennis forehand. A batter is turned away from the pitcher's delivery. The swing is executed with a turn and arm extension toward and through the ball. The one-handed backhand drive, however, has an initial turn but the body remains sideways throughout the contact and follow-through phases. A two-handed backhand closely parallels a forehand drive in its execution.

The forehand and backhand drives can be divided into three major phases of movement: PREPARATION, CONTACT, and FOLLOW-THROUGH. The preparation phase is divided further into the GRIP, READY POSITION and INITIAL REACTION.

THE FOREHAND DRIVE

PREPARATION PHASE

Of the three phases of the forehand drive, the preparation phase is by far the most important. If the racquet is not placed in the proper position to begin with, it is more difficult to achieve the proper position to contact the ball.

The Grip

The Eastern forehand grip is the most common grip used, and should be the preferred grip used by beginners. It keeps the racquet face vertical to the ground so that the center of the strings is more likely to make contact with the ball.

The Eastern forehand grip sometimes is referred to as the "shake hands" grip. The hand is placed on the racquet as though shaking hands with someone (Figure 3.1). The palm of the hand is placed along the flat side of the racquet with the heel of the hand on the butt end of the racquet. The knuckle of the index finger is on the side bevel. The fingers are spread with the index finger acting as a "trigger". A "V" is formed between the thumb and index finger with the point of the "V" directed toward the right shoulder. Although there are other grips that can be used for the forehand drive, the Eastern grip is the classic grip.

Figure 3.1 *Eastern forehand grip.*

Ready Position

In the ready position, the body is balanced and stable (Figure 3.2). It must be balanced to allow movement to be

Figure 3.2 *Ready position--weighted.*

initiated equally in any direction. The shoulders should be square to the net, the trunk leaning slightly forward, and the knees slightly bent. The weight should be evenly distributed over the balls of both feet. The racquet should be directly in front of and away from the body and pointing toward the net. This is the neutral position from which the forehand or backhand can be played. The throat of the racquet should be resting in the non-racquet hand. For the two-handed backhand, both hands should be on the grip. Eyes should be focused in the direction of the ball.

A misleading conception of the ready position is its function in preparation for the return of the ball. The ready position just described is the one which is assumed prior to the server's windup. Because the ready position is a relatively stable position, it sacrifices mobility. In order to move quickly toward the ball, the body must be placed in a position where some of the stability of the body is lost. This is done by unweighting (Figure 3.3).

Checklist for the ready position

_____ shoulders square to the net

_____ trunk in an upright vertical position

_____ knees slightly bent

_____ weight evenly distributed over balls of both feet

_____ racquet in front of and away from the body pointing toward the net

_____ throat of racquet resting in non-racquet hand/both hands on grip in two-handed backhand

_____ eyes focused on the ball

Figure 3.3 *Ready position—unweighted.*

Unweighting occurs when the body wishes to begin a shift in position. The knees are bent less, the feet "lighten" (take quick small steps in place), and the back straightens. This is similar is baseball or softball where the defensive players assume a weighted position prior to the pitcher's windup. Upon delivery, all defensive players move to an unweighted position for quicker movement to the hit ball. Moving the body from a low position to a high position makes it easier to move. The less stability one has the greater the mobility.

Initial Reaction

The initial reaction to the oncoming ball is a step with the rear foot toward a position parallel to the baseline and aligned with the anticipated bounce of the ball. At the same time the step is taken, the entire body turns to a position sideways to the net (Figure 3.4). The body and racquet arm should act as one compact unit. A beginner who uses a long backswing tends to lose the continuity of the motion. In other words, the timing at the point of ball contact is not synchronized with the forward rotation of the body and the forward transfer of the weight. A compact, short backswing places the racquet in the proper position with the weight on the back foot in preparation for the forward transfer of weight and ultimate contact with the ball. The body acts much like a coiled spring ready to be unwound. The unwinding action with the arm and body as one unit is what provides the power for the return of the ball deep into the opponent's court.

Figure 3.4 *Forehand--initial reaction.*

Checklist for the initial reaction

____ step-turn

____ body sideways to the net with weight on back foot

____ racquet and shoulder stay together as one unit

____ shoulder and racquet on same level

____ trunk remains in erect position

____ racquet parallel to ground

____ racquet face angle vertical to ground

____ back foot lined up with ball

____ body set below the ball by bending at the knees

Secondly, this winding action allows for a wider and longer arc to the swing. Theoretically the ball should remain in contact with the racquet for a longer period of time with a resultant increase in the generation of ball power. One can readily see how much power and control is lost when there is no turning action of the body, and the ball is slapped at with just the forearm and wrist.

The path of the racquet arm ultimately determines where the ball will be contacted on the strings of the racquet and the direction the ball will take as it leaves the racquet face. To insure solid contact of the ball on the strings of the racquet, the ball must be hit in the center. Placing the racquet in position to hit the center of the strings is essential. To do this, the racquet should follow the shoulder movement from the ready position to a position directly in line with the shoulders and about shoulder high during the backswing. The free hand should be on the same level as the racquet hand while the trunk is maintained in an upright position. The racquet path should be parallel to the ground, and the racquet face angle should be vertical to the ground. For the ball to clear the net, the body should be set below the ball by bending at the knees. This will create a natural low to high swing.

An additional comment should be made about the footwork involved in the initial reaction to the ball. The basic pattern of movement is to step with the racquet side foot in the direction of the oncoming ball. For example, if the ball is coming directly at you, the step will need to be taken away from the line of the ball. If the ball is a short distance from you and just out of reach, you will need to step outward in the direction of the ball first and then take small steps until you can contact the ball. If the ball is some distance from you, step outward and sprint to reach the ball.

CONTACT PHASE

The contact phase of the forehand drive begins with a front foot stride in the direction of the ball and the net. The unwinding of the body immediately follows the stride (Figure 3.5). This produces the power which will be needed to propel the ball over the net. In order to produce the most efficient power, the unwinding action must occur sequentially. This means that the feet, legs, and hips must initiate the rotation forward toward the net. The trunk, shoulders, arms, and racquet must then follow in sequence.

Figure 3.5 *Forehand--weight transfer.*

Hip and shoulder rotation should be in the direction of the step and the forward movement of the racquet. The racquet should be lowered to a waist or hip high position and parallel to the ground. When you are relaxed, this happens naturally. Remember that the racquet should be working with the rotation and not independent of the rotation. Your head remains stationary with the eyes concentrating on the ball throughout the contact phase. The free hand is working at the same level and in the same direction as the racquet hand. This keeps the body balanced and allows the racquet to be brought to the ball in the proper position. Contact with the ball is made even with the front foot and about a racquet's length away from the body (Figure 3.6).

Checklist for the contact phase

_____ stride toward the net

_____ rotation initiated with hips and back leg

_____ racquet at hip or waist level parallel to ground

_____ racquet strings facing direction of intended hit

_____ head stationary, eyes on ball

_____ free hand working with racquet hand

_____ ball contact even with front foot, racquet length away from body

Figure 3.6   *Forehand--weight transfer and contact.*

FOLLOW-THROUGH PHASE

The follow-through on any of the strokes serves three purposes. First, the follow-through motion allows for a gradual slowing down of the arm rather than coming to an abrupt stop. In this way, an injury to the shoulder and arm could be avoided. Second, the follow-through causes the arm and racquet to maintain speed throughout the contact phase. Earlier it was mentioned that a wide arc of the swing is desirable in generating power. A follow-through motion assures the continuation of the stroke and thus, the speed of the racquet through the ball. Third, the follow-through motion provides for a visual or kinesthetic (feel) feedback of the entire motion. The position of the racquet at the finish should tell you whether your preparation and initial reaction to the ball were done properly, and that when contact with the ball was made all the power generated during rotation and forward transfer of weight was not lost.

The racquet in the forehand drive should continue in the direction you intend for the ball to take as it crosses the net into the opposite court (Figure 3.7). Even though the weight is on the front foot, the back foot should remain on the ground through contact and follow-through. This provides a base to work from and keeps the body in line with the intended target.

Checklist for the follow-through phase

_____ racquet continues along line of ball movement

_____ back foot remains on ground

_____ body rotated to face net

Figure 3.7 *Forehand--follow-through.*

THE BACKHAND DRIVE

The one-handed backhand drive is the classic tennis stroke. Although the fundamental mechanics are relatively easy, the timing is more difficult.

The two-handed backhand drive has become popular in recent years. Its advantage is in the added strength for racquet control. Its limitation is in the reduction of the range of movement permitted and its lack of versatility.

PREPARATION PHASE

As was seen in the forehand drive, the preparation phase is the most important phase of the total movement. Proper preparation should result in good racquet position at contact.

The Grip

The Eastern backhand grip is the classic grip used for a one-handed backhand drive. The position of the hand in the Eastern backhand grip is shifted one-quarter turn to the left or in a counter-clockwise direction for right handed players (See

Figure 3.8). The knuckle of the index finger is now on top of the handle. The fingers should remain spread. The "V" formed between the thumb and index finger now lies in the middle of the bevel of the racquet.

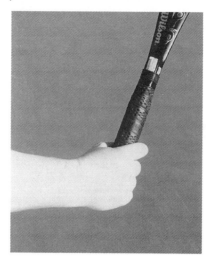

Figure 3.8 *Eastern backhand grip.*

Two-handed Grip

The two-handed backhand stroke is recommended for players who need additional strength and control. This is not an exclusive stroke for these individuals, however, as players of all skill levels have adopted it. Two hands are placed on the racquet close together so that the left hand is in a position above the right hand for right handed players. The left hand is placed on the racquet using the left-handed Eastern forehand grip while the right hand is placed on the racquet also using the right-handed Eastern forehand grip (Figure 3.9). The right hand is used for support while the left hand actually produces the stroke as if hitting a left-handed forehand.

Ready Position

The ready position for the one-handed backhand drive is the same as it was for the forehand drive (Figure 3.2). The ready position for the two-handed backhand has a slightly different placement for the hands on the racquet. Both hands are placed on the grip of the racquet. Refer to the checklist for important reminders in the ready position.

Figure 3.9   *Two-handed backhand grip.*

Checklist for the ready position

_____ shoulders square to the net

_____ trunk in an upright vertical position

_____ knees slightly bent

_____ weight evenly distributed over balls of both feet

_____ racquet directly in front of and away from the body pointing toward the net

_____ throat of racquet resting in non-racquet hand (one-handed backhand)

_____ hands together on grip (two-handed backhand)

_____ eyes focused in direction of oncoming ball

Initial Reaction

The basic step and turn principle employed in the forehand drive applies to the backhand drive. The initial step toward the ball is made with the back foot. The racquet was brought back to shoulder level in the forehand drive and it is pulled to the shoulder on the one-handed backhand drive (Figure 3.10). The two-handed backhand is pulled to the hip (Figure 3.11). The non-racquet hand assists with bringing the racquet back to the shoulder position in the one-handed backhand. Both hands are used to bring the racquet back to the hip in the two-handed backhand.

Figure 3.10 *One-handed backhand -- initial reaction.*

Figure 3.11 *Two-handed backhand -- initial reaction.*

Once again, as in the forehand drive, the racquet must be moving on a line parallel to the ground with the racquet face vertical to the ground. Keeping the trunk in an upright position balances the body and keeps the racquet swinging in an arc parallel to the ground. Refer to the checklist for further reminders of the initial reaction phase.

Checklist for the initial reaction

_____ step-turn

_____ body sideways to the net with weight on back foot

_____ pull racquet to shoulder with the left hand, hip with two hands

_____ trunk remains in an erect position

_____ racquet face angle vertical to ground

_____ line up ball with back foot

_____ set the body below the ball by bending at the knees

CONTACT PHASE FOR ONE-HANDED BACKHAND

There is one important difference between the backhand drive and forehand drive during the contact phase. Remember in the forehand drive, the legs and hips initiated the uncoiling action with the trunk, shoulders, and racquet arm following. In the one-handed backhand, the racquet arm pulls through from the shoulder, but *no* body rotation occurs. The racquet arm is pulled away from the body while the non-racquet arm goes back. All other phases of the movement are similar to the forehand drive. A stride forward is made toward the net with the racquet parallel to the ground (Figure 3.12). The head should remain stationary with the eyes concentrating on the ball throughout the contact phase. Contact with the ball is made even with the front foot about a racquet's length away from the body.

Refer to the checklist for other reminders on how to execute the backhand drive.

Checklist for the One-Handed Backhand Contact Phase

_____ stride forward toward the net

_____ racquet arm pulls from shoulder, no body rotation

_____ non-racquet arm goes back as racquet arm is pulled forward

_____ racquet at hip level parallel to ground

_____ head stationary, eyes on ball

_____ racquet strings facing line of intended hit

_____ ball contact even with front foot racquet length away from body

Figure 3.12 *One-handed backhand-- weight transfer and contact.*

CONTACT PHASE FOR TWO-HANDED BACKHAND

The two-handed backhand drive parallels the forehand drive from the point where the weight is transferred forward to the contact of the ball and the uncoiling of the body occurs. The back arm of the two-handed backhand drive functions in a similar manner to the hitting arm in the forehand drive. The step is made toward the net with the racquet parallel to the ground along the line of flight of the ball. The head should remain stationary with the eyes concentrating on the ball (Figure 3.13). Contact with the ball needs to be made even with the front leg about a racquet's length away from the body (Figure 3.14).

Figure 3.13 *Two-handed backhand-- weight transfer.*

Figure 3.14 *Two-handed backhand-- contact.*

Checklist for the Two-Handed Backhand Contact Phase

_____ stride forward toward the net

_____ rotation initiated with legs and hips

_____ racquet at hip or waist level parallel to ground

_____ swing with back arm

_____ trunk remains in an erect position

_____ racquet strings facing intended target

_____ head stationary with eyes on ball

_____ set body below the ball by bending at the knees

_____ back foot in line with the ball

FOLLOW-THROUGH PHASE

The follow-through for the one-handed and two-handed backhand is the same as it was for the forehand. Basically, the follow-through should finish in a position so that the racquet is aimed in the direction of the intended line of ball flight (Figures 3.15 and 3.16). Refer to the checklist for reminders on the follow-through.

Figure 3.15 *One-handed backhand-- follow-through.*

Figure 3.16 *Two-handed backhand-- follow-through.*

Checklist for the follow-through phase

_____ racquet should continue along line of intended ball movement

_____ back foot remains on ground

SERVE AND VOLLEY:
Back to the Basics

The serve and volley strokes complete what commonly are referred to as the basic strokes in tennis. The other two are the forehand and backhand drives which were discussed in Chapter 3.

THE SERVE

Many consider the serve to be the most important stroke in tennis because it begins every point in every game. This means that the server takes the offensive position and can direct the play of the game. The advantage in play belongs to the server since he/she can control the direction, placement, and speed of the shot. Typically, it is the third stroke to be taught.

Teaching the serve can be expedited by relating the motion to one which is familar to everyone, the overhand throwing motion. Every tennis player at some point in his/her life has picked up an object and thrown it. The overhand throwing motion is considered to be one of the fundamental locomotor patterns developed early in life and later modified into a specific sports skill such as the tennis serve.

The basic throwing motion is one in which the entire body rotates away from the target with the weight on the back foot. Then with an uncoiling action a shift of weight is made in the forward direction. The legs and hips initiate the uncoiling with the trunk and shoulders following sequentially. The upper arm, elbow, and wrist are the last segments to come forward in a whipping-like action. The wrist snaps forward toward the target releasing the held object. The serving motion follows a similar basic pattern as throwing. The same weight transference, uncoiling, and whip-like action at the wrist occurs as the racquet is brought forward to make contact with the ball. The serve can be divided into the following phases of movement: PREPARATION, WIND-UP, CONTACT, and FOLLOW-THROUGH.

PREPARATION PHASE

The Grip

Two grips may be used for the serve. The Eastern forehand grip (Figure 3.1) is the preferred grip by beginners or players who desire to hit a "flat" serve because it positions the racquet face in line with the target. The ball can be hit squarely in the center of the strings, and is projected forward with very little spin.

The Continental grip or the Eastern backhand generally is considered to be the grip used by more advanced players(Figure 4.1). The Continental grip allows for greater wrist action and places the racquet face in a position to put more spin on the ball. For the Continental grip the hand is placed midway between the Eastern forehand and the Eastern backhand grip. The knuckle of the index finger lies halfway between the top of the handle and the first bevel to the right (referred to as the ridge) of the handle.

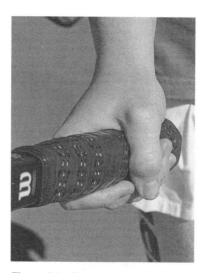

Figure 4.1 *Continental grip.*

Stance and Body Position

The preparation phase for the serve is concerned with the stance and body position. The feet, hip, shoulders, and racquet should be lined up in a sideways or perpendicular position with the target area (Figure 4.2).

This allows the body, arm, and racquet path to be aligned with the intended path of the ball flight. Also, this places the body in an optimal position for power and accuracy. The feet should be shoulder width apart. The weight should be on the back foot. The racquet should be in front of the body with the tip pointing toward the target. The throat of the racquet rests in the non-racquet (tossing) hand.

Checklist for the preparation phase

_____ feet, hip, shoulder, racquet lined up sideways with target area

_____ feet shoulder width apart

_____ weight on back foot

_____ racquet in front of body in direction of target

_____ non-racquet hand holding on to throat of racquet

Figure 4.2 *Serve--preparation, stance, weight back.*

WIND-UP PHASE

Remember the ultimate goal in the serve is speed with accuracy. To develop the desired optimized speed in the racquet at contact, acceleration must begin during the wind-up phase. Over the course of the winding action each part of the body contributes to this build up of speed in a sequential fashion. This is sometimes referred to in sports as "good timing". In the wind-up, emphasis should be placed on making the motion fluid and slow through the release of the ball toss with a gradual speed increase. A hurried motion tends to disrupt the "timing" with a resultant loss in speed at ball contact.

The first move in the wind-up phase is the dropping of both hands simultaneously. When the hands approach the front knee, they separate much like they do when performing a jumping jack exercise (Figure 4.3). The racquet arm rotates outward at the shoulder as the racquet is drawn backward. If the arm is relaxed, the outward arm rotation occurs naturally resulting in an open racquet face. Figure 4.4 shows this open position of the racquet face. The weight now begins to shift upward and forward. The weight shift corresponds to the toss arm position. The arms continue in their wide circular motion. The ball is released when the non-racquet hand reaches a peak above the head and just in front of the forward foot in line with the optimal contact point. The hands work in unison and upon release of the ball, the arms appear to be in a V-position. The racquet continues its circular motion until it reaches a cocked position behind the back. This often is referred to as the "back-scratch" position (Figure 4.5).

The height of the ball toss is a controlled *slow, fluid* wind-up motion. At its peak, the ball needs to be only as high as you can extend your racquet.

Figure 4.3 *Serve--wind-up, drop hands.*

Figure 4.4 *Serve--toss, weight balanced.*

Checklist for the wind-up phase

_____ hand drop simultaneously

_____ weight is on back foot

_____ hands separate as front knee is approached

_____ racquet face opens after hands separate

_____ weight shifts up and forward with toss

_____ ball released when non-racquet hand reaches peak above head and in front of forward foot

_____ V-position of arms at ball release

_____ ball toss height equal to height of racquet extension

_____ racquet in back-scratch position

Figure 4.5 *Serve--back-scratch position.*

CONTACT PHASE

For optimum results, a continuous movement of the racquet from the drop of the hands to the follow-through is necessary. As the racquet is brought upward from the cocked position ("back-scratch") behind the back, it appears to be thrown at the ball. This implies that the ball should be hit upward and not downward. You would need to be almost 7 feet tall to hit the ball on a downward trajectory and have it clear the net (Figure 4.6). The weight continues to move forward. The racquet face should be facing the

target area which means the racquet face and palm of the hand should be facing the correct service court. The head remains up while the eyes continue to look at the ball *through contact*. Avoid looking down the court to see where the ball has landed.

Checklist for the contact phase

____ racquet thrown at ball

____ hit up on ball

____ weight forward

____ racquet strings facing target area

____ head stationary and looking at ball

Figure 4.6 *Serve--contact, hit up on the ball.*

FOLLOW-THROUGH PHASE

Providing the ball toss is in the proper place and the racquet has accelerate *through* the ball, a natural follow-through should terminate the action. This means that the racquet arm will cross the body and begin to decelerate. The back foot will have continued its forward motion into the court (Figure 4.7).

Checklist for the follow-through phase

____ racquet arm across body

____ weight forward

Figure 4.7 *Serve--follow-through.*

THE VOLLEY

The volley stroke is defined as a ball which is hit before it touches the ground. There are defensive and offensive volleys. Defensive volleys are hit from a position farther from the net than offensive volleys. These volleys are usually below net level making it harder to control. Being closer to the net makes it easier to make contact with the ball above net level. There is less chance of hitting the ball into the net. Also from closer, the ball can be directed toward any part of the opponent's court. This is a good offensive weapon because: (a) it gives the opponent less time to react to the shot; (b) it forces the opponent to hit perfectly placed passing shots; and (c) it gives the offensive player the opportunity to hit angled shots anywhere on the court.

The volley can be divided into two main phases: the PREPARATION and CONTACT. There is no follow-through phase for the volley except to remain in the balanced contact position making sure the weight goes through the volley.

PREPARATION PHASE

The Grip

The Continental grip is recommended for the volley stroke. This previously was described for the serve (Figure 4.1). Because the reaction to the ball must be made quickly, there is little time to be concerned with changing from a forehand to a backhand grip or vice versa. The Continental grip permits a player to hit either a forehand or backhand volley with the same grip. Equally as important is the slightly open angle of the racquet face which is the natural result of the Continental grip. The advantage of an angled racquet is a better chance for the ball to clear the net and the natural slice which is placed on the ball. The slice does take some power off the ball, but the major advantage is in better control of ball placement into the opponent's court. The slice slows the ball creating a lower bounce which makes it more difficult for the opposing player to execute a passing shot.

The preparation phase, with the exception of the grip, is the same as it was for the groundstrokes (Refer to Chapter 3). That is, the shoulders are square to the net, trunk straight, and the knees slightly bent. The weight should be evenly distributed over the balls of both feet. The racquet should be directly in front of and away from the body and with the tip pointing toward the net. The throat of the racquet should be resting in the non-racquet hand. The two-handed backhand volley ready position should be prepared with a two-handed backhand grip. Eyes should be focused on the ball at all times.

Checklist for the preparation phase

_____ shoulders square to the net

_____ trunk straight

_____ knees slightly bent

_____ weight evenly distributed over balls of both feet

_____ racquet directly in front of and away from body pointing toward net

_____ throat of racquet resting in non-racquet hand/ 2-handed grip

_____ eyes focused on the ball

CONTACT PHASE

The opposite foot and both hands react toward the ball simultaneously in the forehand volley (Figure 4.8). The step with the opposite foot will direct the body at an angle to the net rather than facing the net. The same side foot reacts toward the ball in the backhand volley. (See Figures 4.9 and 4.10). There is *no* backswing in the volley stroke because the force of the oncoming ball will supply its own power off the racquet. Additionally, the weight transfer and solid immovable racquet face give the ball all the power and direction it will need. The less the racquet moves, the more control is permitted, thus minimizing the margin for error.

Figure 4.8 *Forehand volley--contact position.*

Figure 4.9 *One-handed backhand volley--contact position.*

Figure 4.10 *Two-handed backhand volley--contact position.*

The racquet in the ready position is approximately shoulder height. This is the strongest and most advantageous position to make contact with the ball and permits the most racquet control. If the ball must be struck from below net height, the knees should be bent to adjust to the ball height (Figure 4.11 and 4.12). Avoid bending at the waist because of the tendency for the body to become unbalanced or unstable resulting in poor racquet control.

Figure 4.11 *Forehand volley--bend knees for low balls.*

Figure 4.12 *Backhand volley--bend knees for low balls.*

Keep the eyes focused on the ball through contact. When contacting the ball, the upper body position is best when it appears to be in the ready position. Make position and weight changes with the legs.

Checklist for the contact phase

_____ opposite foot and both hands react toward ball simultaneously

_____ no backswing

_____ minimum racquet movement

_____ racquet head stationary

_____ eyes on ball through contact

_____ knees bent to reach balls beneath net height

FOLLOW-THROUGH PHASE

There is no follow through phase such as seen in the forehand or backhand drives. Rather, the body and racquet move forward as one unit with the strings facing the intended ball direction.

Chapter 5

ADVANCED STROKES:
Overhead, Lob, Approach, Dropshot, Spins, Return of Serve

Once the basic groundstrokes have been mastered, variations of those strokes can be learned. These advanced strokes are the overhead, lob, approach shot, drop shot, spins, and return of serve. Similarities exist between the stroke mechanics of the basic strokes and the advanced strokes.

THE OVERHEAD

The overhead is a forceful offensive shot used to answer a lob. It is used when the ball is high enough to fully extend the racquet and arm above the head for contact. This stroke is sometimes referred to as the "smash". The major phases of the overhead are: INITIAL REACTION, CONTACT, and FOLLOW-THROUGH.

INITIAL REACTION PHASE

As in all previous discussions of stroke mechanics, a proper initial reaction is essential if a player hopes to be successful. The first movement, therefore, needs to be a step and turn with the back foot positioned parallel to the net. At the same time, the hands are raised above the head (Figure 5.1). Remember this is all *one motion*.

Figure 5.1 *Overhead--initial reaction.*

The weight remains on the back foot while the elbow bends placing the racquet in a back-scratch position. The timing of the stroke does not allow for a full wind-up or cock position of the racquet. The non-racquet arm remains up in the air reaching or pointing toward the ball. This keeps the shoulders sideways to the net.

The back foot needs to be positioned about three feet behind and to the side of the point at which the ball will be contacted. A point should be picked out as you watch the flight arc of the ball. When you step forward to meet the ball, the contact point will be the point where the arm and racquet can be fully extended.

Checklist for the initial reaction phase

_____ step and turn, weight back

_____ hands above head

_____ elbow bend to back-scratch

_____ non-racquet hand pointing toward ball

_____ racquet side foot 3 feet behind and side of contact point

CONTACT PHASE

The contact phase is initiated with a step forward with the front leg. The non-racquet arm pulls down and back to set up a reaction with the hitting arm. As the non-racquet arm is drawn back, the body begins a turning motion toward the net, thus accelerating the racquet. This turning motion is the source of the power surge for the stroke. The racquet is "thrown" upward and through the ball with the arm in full extension (Figure 5.2). This allows the ball to follow a better trajectory over the net.

Checklist for the contact phase

_____ step forward with the front foot

_____ throw racquet upward toward ball

_____ contact ball at full arm extension

Figure 5.2 *Overhead--contact.*

FOLLOW-THROUGH PHASE

After contact with the ball has been made, there should be a feeling of "throwing" the racquet to a spot on the opponent's court. The racquet should end up across the body (Figure 5.3).

Checklist for the follow-through phase

_____ throw racquet to a spot on opponent's court

_____ racquet finishes across the body

_____ right foot steps forward

Figure 5.3 *Follow-through*

THE LOB

The lob is a high arched "touch" shot which can be used as either an offensive or defensive shot. As an offensive shot it is used to move an opponent away from the net and toward the baseline. This removes him/her from an advantageous offensive position at the net. As a defensive shot, the lob is used as a time-saver. If you are out of position to hit a return, the lob can be hit to allow you more time to recover in preparation for the next shot.

The major phases of the lob shot are: INITIAL   REACTION, CONTACT, and FOLLOW-THROUGH.

INITIAL REACTION PHASE

The initial reaction phase for the lob is exactly as it was for the forehand and backhand drives. The one main difference is that the racquet face must be in an open position with the strings of the racquet pointing upward (Figure 5.4). Refer to Chapter 3 for complete descriptions of the forehand and backhand drives.

Figure 5.4 *Lob--contact with open racquet face.*

Checklist for the initial reaction phase

_____ step and turn

_____ body sideways to the net with weight on back foot

_____ trunk remains in erect position

_____ open racquet face position

_____ body set below the ball by bending at the knees

CONTACT PHASE

The weight transfer is the same as it is for the forehand and backhand drives. The contact phase is characterized by the racquet contact on the bottom of the ball with the racquet face remaining open. The path of the racquet should follow the intended path of the ball. A good player can disguise this shot by preparing initially like a groundstroke and opening the racquet face early in the contact phase.

Checklist for the contact phase

_____ stride forward toward the net

_____ racquet face in open position

_____ contact ball on bottom

FOLLOW-THROUGH PHASE

The racquet should continue moving in the intended line of ball flight. Remember that with the racquet strings in an open position, the path of the racquet will be directed upward (Figure 5.5).

Figure 5.5 *Lob--follow-through with open racquet face.*

Checklist for the follow-through phase

_____ racquet continues in intended path of ball

APPROACH/ HALF-VOLLEY

The approach shot is made most often when the opponent's ball has been hit somewhere near the service line. The purpose of the shot is to approach the net to assume an offensive position. Success at the net is directly dependent upon the quality of the approach shot. An approach shot hit deep (close to opponent's baseline) is a quality shot. It is hit just like the forehand and backhand drives with one exception, the backswing is shortened (Figures 5.6 and 5.7). Refer to Chapter 3 on the basic groundstrokes for a refresher on the execution of these strokes.

Figure 5.6 *Forehand approach/half volley--short backswing.*

Figure 5.7 *Backhand approach/half volley--short backswing.*

The backswing must be shortened to facilitate better timing for control and accuracy. This is necessary since there is less court to work with. A critical part of this stroke is the amount of time the ball stays on the racquet. The half volley is a shot hit immediately after the ball hits the court. This shot is executed like the approach shot. Make sure to stay low to the court with knees bent and racquet low while executing the half volley. (Figures 5.8 and 5.9)

Figure 5.8 *Forehand approach/ half volley--contact.*

Figure 5.9 *Backhand approach/ half volley--contact.*

Checklist for the approach/half-volley

_____ same as forehand and backhand

_____ shortened backswing

_____ keep the ball on the strings (Figures 5.10 and 5.11)

_____ stay low

Figure 5.10 *Forehand approach/half volley--follow-through.*   **Figure 5.11** *Backhand approach/half volley--follow-through.*

THE DROP SHOT

The drop shot requires the most racquet control of any shot in tennis. This shot is often referred to as a "touch shot". It is used to place the ball in the forecourt, near the net, and out of the reach of an opponent. It is effective when used against players who favor baseline, or groundstroke shots. It is a somewhat difficult shot to master because it requires precision timing, accuracy, and racquet control. Also it is a seldom practiced shot.

The major phases of the drop shot are: INITIAL REACTION, CONTACT, and FOLLOW-THROUGH.

INITIAL REACTION PHASE

The first movement in the initial reaction phase is a step and turn with the weight being placed on the back foot. The backswing is a *short* one. It is extremely important that the hands work as one unit, on one level, and in one direction. This stroke needs good balance and racquet control (Figure 5.12). It is very much like the preparation for the approach shot.

Figure 5.12 *Forehand drop shot-- balance.*

Checklist for the initial reaction phase

_____ step and turn

_____ short backswing

_____ weight on back foot

_____ hands working as one unit

CONTACT PHASE

The power of the ball must be absorbed by "cradling" the ball on the racquet face which is in an open position. The term "soft hands" often is used to describe this action. The body must be balanced, so the weight needs to go forward and turn slowly with the knees slightly bent. Once the speed of the ball has been absorbed, it should be lifted as if hitting a "mini" lob. The vertical lift will keep the ball close to the net rather than being projected deep down court. (Figure 5.13)

Figure 5.13 *Backhand drop shot--contact.*

Checklist for the contact phase

_____ step and turn slowly

_____ "cradle" ball

FOLLOW-THROUGH PHASE

The racquet should continue moving in the intended line of ball flight. There should be a feeling of "lifting" the ball and carefully laying the ball into the other court. (Figures 5.14 and 5.15)

Figure 5.14 *Forehand drop shot--follow-through.*

Figure 5.15 *Backhand drop shot--follow-through*

Checklist for the follow-through phase

_____ racquet moving in direction of ball

_____ lay ball into opponent's court

_____ think "soft"

SPINS

Spin alters the direction and speed characteristics of a rebounding ball. Advanced tennis players include the use of spins in their repertoire of shots to gain an advantage over their opponents. The two primary types of spin are the slice and topspin. The slice is used especially on approach shots for the purpose of getting the ball to skid and bounce low.

The initial reaction for a sliced groundstroke mirrors a flat drive except for the height and angle of the racquet face. That is, the racquet should be head high with an open face (Figures 5.16 and 5.19). The racquet should drive through the ball (Figures 5.17 and 5.20). The finish is head high with the racquet face open (Figures 5.18 and 5.21). The path of the racquet looks like a long drawn out "U".

Figure 5.16 *Slice forehand -- open racquet face, initial reaction.*

Figure 5.17 *Slice forehand -- open racquet face,weight transfer, contact*

Figure 5.18 *Slice forehand -- follow-through*

Figure 5.19 *Slice backhand -- open racquet face, initial reaction.*

Figure 5.20 *Slice backhand -- open racquet face, initial contact.*

Figure 5.21 *Slice backhand -- open racquet face, follow-through.*

A common error of a slice is not finishing the follow-through. This is considered a "chop" in stead of a drive. The result is a high floating ball. A second common error is wrist collapse. The result is a slow floating ball.

Topspin takes more work and time to produce, but it creates a better margin for error. The low to high hitting style gives the ball a more arched path. The spin acted on by gravity allows the ball to drop more quickly. This combination makes the ball bounce higher after contact with the court. To produce the forehand and backhand shots effectively, the initial reaction must be altered. As the step and turn sequence is taken, the elbow is bent and raised to shoulder height (Figures 5.22 and 5.25a) The racquet in this position is closed and facing the ground (Figure 5.25b). The back knee and shoulder are dropped to get the racquet below the ball. The same knee and shoulder are driven to and through the ball (Figures 5.23 and 5.26). The follow-through will be high with a closed racquet face (Figures 5.24 and 5.27). Common errors are swing with the lower arm creating a weaker and more erratic result, a sloppy racquet face (slapping), and failing to fully rotate the shoulders sideways when using and open stance.

Figure 5.22 *Topspin forehand - closed racquet face, initial reaction*

Figure 5.23 *Topspin forehand -- contact*

Figure 5.24 *Topspin forehand --
follow-through*

Figure 5.25a *Topspin backhand --
initial reaction*

Figure 5.25b *Topspin backhand --
closed racquet face*

Figure 5.26 *Topspin backhand --
slightly closed racquet face,contact*

Figure 5.27 *Topspin backhand --
follow-through*

SERVICE RETURN

The return of serve most resembles an approach shot. Because the serve is considered an offensive shot and has considerable speed on it, there is less time to prepare for the return. The shortened backswing provides an opportunity to hit the ball earlier which, along with the follow-through, controls the return.

One more important aspect of the service return is the footwork. Once the server begins the windup, the returner "unweights" and begins moving the feet. This gives the body a chance to react more quickly.

Chapter 6

ANALYSIS OF TENNIS STROKES

One of the most difficult tasks a teacher faces in teaching tennis is the analysis of the stroke patterns. How do you know what to look for first in efficient stroke mechanics, and then how do you relay this information to the player? To the "trained" observer this is relatively easy, but to the "untrained" eye, this can be frustrating. The player expects immediate help in perfecting his/her stroke, and you as a teacher should know what to emphasize first. Secondly, what cues can you provide for the player so that he/she can "feel" the correct movement pattern and experience success?

Ideally, every teacher would have at his/her disposal a high speed motion picture camera or videotape machine which would slow the action of the tennis strokes for a frame-by-frame analysis. This is an unrealistic expectation in most situations however, and so the teacher must rely on the next best camera available, the "naked eye". In this chapter, a time-tested method of systematically analyzing each tennis stroke with naked eye observations will be described. Key points for observation will be discussed. For a complete description of each stroke, refer back to Chapters 3 and 4. The major focus will be on: a) which phases of the movement should receive the most concentration; b) typical errors; c) reasoning behind the suggested corrections; and d) teaching cues.

THE FOREHAND ANALYSIS

The first thing observed in the execution of the forehand drive is not necessarily the major problem of the stroke. For example, the follow-through action of an improperly executed forehand is the easiest observation to make because it is what the eyes see last in the movement. The action prior to the follow-through happens so quickly that the "untrained" eye cannot always pick up the subtle incorrect movements which are being made. One inefficient move added to another adds up to a gross error, usually noticeable in the follow-through.

If errors can be cumulative, then it would seem only reasonable that the first chance for an incorrect move to occur would be in the initial reaction phase. It is important, therefore, that the teacher concentrate on the first movements of the player.

INITIAL REACTION PHASE

The first and most important movement to look for in the initial reaction phase is the step with the racquet side foot parallel to the baseline and the shoulder turn with the racquet coming back as one unit (Figure 6.1). The power for the stroke comes from upper body rotation. This allows for an expanded hitting zone, and allows for the racquet to hit through the ball. The longer the racquet remains on the ball the greater the power generated and the greater the control of the ball into the opposite court.

Figure 6.1 *Initial reaction phase, step-turn*

A common error in this first reaction to the ball is a failure to turn the shoulders so that the body is parallel to the sideline with the racquet being brought back as one unit with the shoulder. If the body is facing toward the net, the wrist must be laid back to allow the racquet strings to face the net so that the ball may be directed into the opposite court. This means that the arm and hand are performing the bulk of the work. As a result, the arc of the racquet path is reduced. This means that power and, more importantly, the control of the ball has been lost.

A second common error is the failure to step toward the ball with the proper timing. Sometimes a pivot is made instead of taking a step with the back foot. This causes an instability of the body and results in the weight being directed forward too early toward the oncoming ball. The rhythm of the stroke is disrupted and the power transmitted to the ball is reduced. The body fails to work in unison with the arms and racquet.

Simple short phrases are the best cues for teaching. It gives the player time to react to the ball without having to spend time thinking through each movement. Cues should also be given early which will allow the player to "feel" the movement. If the movement cannot be felt, it cannot be reproduced at will. In the initial reaction phase just described, a cue such as "STEP-TURN" should get the point across to the player.

Once the initial step-turn movement has been made and observed, the next movement to be focused on should be the racquet path. As the racquet is brought back, it should remain shoulder high (Figure 6.1). The resultant racquet path will enable the timing to be perfect for ball contact. Also it will allow more time for the racquet to act on the ball so that it can generate power and enhance control.

Dropping the racquet head causes an inefficient racquet path and increases the chance for a miss-hit ball. The path of the racquet should follow a small arc in the preparation phase and then a gradually ascending line through the ball during the contact phase. If the racquet head has been dropped initially, the path looks more like a "V" (Figure 6.2). The player will most likely hit down on the ball or up on the ball because of the misdirected racquet path. The result is little or no movement of the racquet through the ball. The ball has a tendency to "fly" off the racquet strings and out of control. Teaching cue: "RACKET WITH SHOULDER".

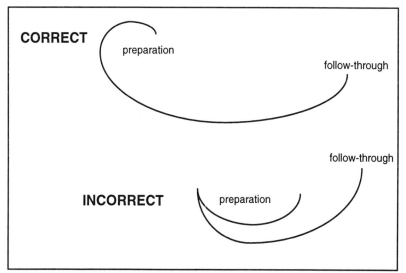

Figure 6.2 *Correct and incorrect racquet paths*

Another key point in the observation of the initial reaction is in the position of the shoulders. They should be level or parallel to the ground which means that the back must also be fairly straight (Figure 6.1). This places the center of gravity over the feet for better balance. The balanced position of the body facilitates the proper racquet path. The non racquet hand also is very important in maintaining balance and keeping the shoulders level. That is, both hands need to work on the same plane and direction. A cue for this sequence of events might be "BACK STRAIGHT" - "WORK HANDS TOGETHER".

Finally, the back foot alignment with the ball is critical. Once again this places the body in optimum position for the greatest racquet efficiency.

CONTACT PHASE

As has been mentioned previously, the shoulder and racquet should work together to produce a smooth, fluid swing. (Figure 6.3) Stopping or slowing down the racquet in the hitting zone will result in lack of control. The sound of the racquet on the ball will give you a clue as to whether the ball has been hit solidly. Your head is the key to observing this motion. If the head remains stationary, the ball has a much better chance of hitting in the middle of the strings. The obvious teaching cue is "HEAD STILL".The racquet and body should come in from below the ball. An appropriate teaching cue for this action would be "LEGS UNDER THE BALL".

Figure 6.3 *Contact phase, racquet with shoulder, balanced.*

FOLLOW-THROUGH PHASE

The follow-through is a product of the initial reaction phase and the contact phase. It should be used as an indicator of a prior mistake in stroking mechanics, but should not be emphasized when teaching. (Figure 6.4)

Figure 6.4 *Follow-through.*

THE BACKHAND ANALYSIS

Just as in the forehand, the follow-through often is the first observable motion by the "untrained" eye. Remember again that the initial movement is the key to the success of the stroke and as such must be focused on first.

INITIAL REACTION PHASE

Recall in Chapter 3 that the description of the initial reaction in the backhand involved a step with the non-racquet side foot parallel to the baseline. The shoulders turned and the racquet came back as one unit (Figures 6.5 and 6.6). This movement should be emphasized as the key to a good stroking pattern. The racquet is pulled back to the shoulder with the help of the non-racquet hand and the weight primarily rests on the back foot. In the two-handed backhand, the racquet is pulled back to the hip with both hands close together on the racquet handle. The teaching cues "STEP-TURN" and "PULL" work quite effectively here.

Figure 6.5 *One-handed backhand--initial reaction phase, step-turn.*

Figure 6.6 *Two-handed backhand--initial reaction.*

Even though the one-handed backhand mechanically is an easier stroke to perform, the timing needs to be correct for the shot to be a success. A forehand or two-handed backhand can be "muscled" when contact of the ball is made late. A typical error in the initial reaction of the preparation phase is moving the racquet back too slowly. Adjustments to the oncoming ball cannot be made in time and contact with the ball is made too late. When the backhand is hit late, the player often tries to rotate the shoulder to get the racquet to the ball. Rotating the shoulders results in an altered racquet path. Hitting late may result in a bent elbow position in which the elbow itself is pointing toward the opposite court. The shortened lever can be moved through the arc of the swing more quickly than can the straight arm long lever. This is the way the body compensates for the late swing. It also is one of the leading causes of tennis elbow, a nagging pain on the outside of the elbow.

It is important for the player to remain balanced throughout the stroking motion to provide for the proper racquet path. The teacher should watch for level shoulders, a straight back, and the center of gravity postioned over the feet or base of support. This is true for the one-handed or two-handed backhand. The teaching cue here is "BACK STRAIGHT - SHOULDERS LEVEL".

CONTACT PHASE

The player should strive for a smooth, fluid swing. There should be no forward body rotation in the one-handed backhand drive. The shoulders should be kept in one place while the swing forward is made with the arm only. There should be a feeling of pulling from the shoulder while the non-racquet hand remains behind (Figure 6.7). Opening up the shoulders to the net alters the path of the racquet. Teaching cues here might be "PULL FROM THE SHOULDER-FREE HAND AWAY".

The two-handed backhand parallels the forehand drive in that the back arm (right-handed player) works with the back shoulder. In addition, the shoulder rotation provides the power source. It is important in this phase that the front upper arm remains close to the body allowing the back arm to perform the stroke. (Figure 6.8) The teaching cue for the two-handed backhand should emphasize the back arm action so the teaching cue here might be "BACK ARM".

Figure 6.7 *One-handed backhand-- weight transfer and contact.*

Figure 6.8 *Two-handed backhand-- balance, turn through like the forehand.*

Finally, if all has gone well up to this point, the observer should look for the racquet and body to come in from below the ball. The head should remain immobile throughout the hit. Teaching cues here might be "LEGS UNDER THE BALL-HEAD STILL".

FOLLOW-THROUGH PHASE

The follow-through is a product of the initial reaction during the preparation phase and the contact phase of the stroke. It should be used as an indicator of a prior mistake in stroking mechanics just as it was in the forehand stroke.

THE SERVE ANALYSIS

The serve is characterized by a slow, rhythmic movement where the hands, racquet, and weight transfer work in unison. The proper alignment of the body in ready position for the start of the motion should be the first checkpoint. The feet, hips, shoulders, and racquet should be aligned in the direction of the intended flight of the ball (Figure 6.9). This is one of the easier things to see because there is no immediate movement involved.

Figure 6.9 *Serve alignment*

THE WIND-UP PHASE

The emphasis on the backswing and wind-up once again is on the slow, smooth rhythm. The hands must work in unison until they reach the "V" position (Figure 6.10). If the rhythm is too fast in the beginning, the timing is disrupted and the continuity of the stroke is lost. The stop and start motion is observed as a jerky motion rather than a smooth flowing one. Key teaching cues might be "DROP, SHIFT, LIFT".

Figure 6.10 *"V" position*

An especially important point during this phase of the serve is the working of the hands in unison. The body then works in unison with the hands. If the hands are working separately, the body becomes confused and does not know which hand should be followed. A teaching cue here might be "HANDS WORK TOGETHER".

Weight transfer should move up through the toss. It is important that the transfer of weight occurs in the knees and ankles instead of the hips. The ball actually is laid up into the air rather than being tossed into the air. If this occurs the ball should be released at the peak of the tossing hand. The racquet then continues its motion into the "back-scratch" position from where it will be accelerated toward the ball (Figure 6.11). "KEEP THE RACKET MOVING IN A LARGE SMOOTH CIRCLE" might be a good cue here. All during this time, the body should be loose and relaxed. It should be remembered that the rhythm and racquet suppy the power, not the muscles of the arm.

Figure 6.11 *Back-scratch position*

CONTACT PHASE

If the downward backswing motion has been a slow, smooth motion, and if the weight transfer forward and upward has been made properly, the racquet should continue to accelerate *through* ball contact. At this time the body and racquet will be fully extended with the eyes focused upward on the ball (Figure 6.12). The player should have a feeling of hitting "up" on the ball. As the ball leaves the racquet there is a slight rising effect. Teaching cues here might be "HIT UP" / "HEAD UP".

Figure 6.12 *Contact, hit up, head up.*

The position of the ball at the peak of the toss should be only as high as the reach of the racquet. If the hands have worked in unison to the "V" position during the backswing and windup phase, the ball will be released at the proper position which is in front of and to the same side of the body as the racquet hand shoulder.

FOLLOW-THROUGH PHASE

Following contact with the ball, the racquet should continue moving downward toward across the body. If the racquet has been accelerated properly, it should end up under the opposite arm. (Figure 6.13)

Figure 6.13 *Let it finish.*

THE VOLLEY ANALYSIS

The key to hitting a successful volley is to make the entire body work as one unit. The right and left hands and the opposite foot should be moving toward the ball together. No backswing should be used in the volley. The contact position looks like the ready position, but the body position is turned at about a 45 degree angle to the net and in the direction of the ball. (Figures 6.14, 6.15 and 6.16).

Figure 6.14 *Forehand volley contact position.*

Figure 6.15 *One handed backhand volley --contact position.*

Figure 6.16   *Two-handed backhand volley -- balanced position.*

There are four common errors in performing the volley. First, if the hands separate, an automatic backswing occurs. When a backswing is used in a volley the resultants quite often are a late contact point, miss-hit, or over hit. Second, the upper body often is used to adjust to the ball rather than the legs. Adjustment with the upper body causes imbalance and ultimately lack of racquet control. Third, a player may wait for the ball to arrive rather than going to meet the ball. Control and positioning are easier to achieve when moving toward a moving object. Fourth, the wrong foot may be used in stepping toward the ball. Stepping with the wrong foot moves the body weight parallel to the net and makes the shoulder turn more difficult. Facing the net in this manner creates the necessity for laying the wrist back in order to contact the ball. Teaching cues which may assist the player in avoiding these errors could be "HANDS TOGETHER" and "GO MEET THE BALL WITH YOUR LEGS".

Chapter 7

DRILLS: Practice Makes Perfect

Drills and practice sessions should be kept functional, and they should simulate game-like situations as much as possible. Likewise, the drills should focus on the stroke mechanics as they will be used during play. This allows the player an opportunity to "feel" the actual motions which will be used in playing, and begin to develop a kinesthetic awareness of their body parts in space.

This chapter will be divided into two parts: practice drills for the individual, and practice drills for groups.

INDIVIDUAL PRACTICE DRILLS

Individual practice drills are done mainly on backboards. In order to make it an effective and worthwhile practice session, one should be aware of a few guidelines. First of all, be sure to stand far enough away from the board, letting the ball bounce twice if necessary, to allow time to think through the stroke mechanics. Secondly, swing through *all the way to the target* to gain ball control.

A ball machine is an excellent practice tool if available. It assists the tennis player in "grooving" stroke mechanics.

GROUNDSTROKES

Several options exist for practicing the forehand and backhand drives against the backboard.

1. Set a target on the wall to the right side of the body for the forehand.
2. Set a target on the wall to the left side of the body for the backhand.
3. Alternate the forehand and backhand by setting a target directly in front of you.

SERVE

The serve can be practiced on a backboard or on the court. The main objective here simply is to line up to a target and attempt to hit that target. Concentration here should be on establishing a slow, fluid rhythm.

The toss for the serve can be practiced anywhere. Recall that the rhythm and the "V" position will dictate the success of the serve because it is the main control for the ball toss.

1. Practice the toss from the ready position to the "V" position. Use a racquet for realistic balancing.
2. Toss the ball into the air and attempt to catch it without moving the tossing hand.

VOLLEY

The volley is a difficult stroke to practice off the back-boards. It is difficult to control, especially for beginning players. Several options can be used.

1. Stand approximately 8 feet from the board and attempt to hit the board as many times as possible without having the ball touch the ground.
2. Start with the groundstrokes, and then move forward until a volley can be made.

COMBINATION STROKES

Serve and play out a point. Plan ahead. Decide where the serve will be executed and then plan the next succession of shots.

GROUP DRILLS

Small and large group practice drills can be organized even with minimal facilities and/or equipment. The key to making the most effective use of time and personnel is organization. This means that every player has a specific duty to perform while the teacher controls the time element.

Generally speaking, it is important that the following be remembered:

1. Each player must have a specific duty to perform.
2. The pattern of rotation should be a logical one. (e.g. in a clockwise direction.)
3. Each player should know how to set the ball up properly to the hitter. This means tossing the ball to a specific spot on the court, with control, and accuracy. (See shaded areas on figures.)
4. Drills should be set up on time intervals rather than upon completion of a set number of hits. This keeps the groups moving along at the same pace for instructional purposes.
5. Stress safety before beginning each drill.
   a. racquet on the ground while explanations are being given
   b. refrain from walking behind or in front of someone who is swinging a racquet
   c. throw or roll the ball to the tosser instead of hitting it to him/her

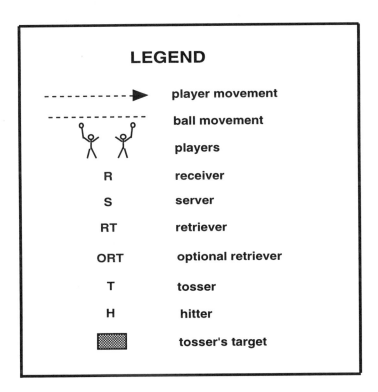

LEGEND

- - - - - - - - - ▶	**player movement**
- - - - - - - - - - ○	**ball movement**
👤 👤	**players**
R	**receiver**
S	**server**
RT	**retriever**
ORT	**optional retriever**
T	**tosser**
H	**hitter**
▓▓▓	**tosser's target**

GROUNDSTROKES (3-5 PLAYERS PER COURT)

Figure 7.1 illustrates the positions for each player in the group. An explanation of positions and responsibilities is described below:

	POSITION	RESPONSIBILITY
Hitter	one step behind baseline facing net	concentrate on stroking ball properly
Tosser	between net and serving line, across net	throw ball to spot between serviceline and base-line to stroke side of hitter
Retriever **#1**	baseline behind tosser	retrieve balls and return to tosser
#2	net on stroke side of court	retrieve balls and return to tosser
#3	baseline opposite corner of #1	retrieve balls and return to tosser

SMALL (3-5)	LARGE (6-10)
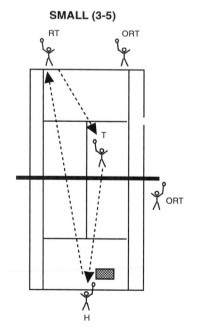	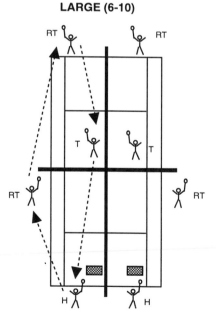
NOTE: For backhands, move tosser to other box	NOTE: For backhands, move players 3'

Figure 7.1 *Groundstrokes, small group*   **Figure 7.2** *Groundstrokes, large group*

GROUNDSTROKES (6-10 PLAYERS PER COURT)

For larger groups, divide the court lengthwise. Assign a group of 3-5 players to each half of a court and proceed with the drills as explained for smaller groups (Figure 7.2).

VOLLEYS (3-5 PLAYERS PER COURT)

Figure 7.3 illustrates the positions for each player in the group. An explanation of positions and responsibilities is described below.

	POSITION	RESPONSIBILITY
Hitter	8 -10 feet from net	Concentrate on proper stroke mechanics
Tosser	Between service line and baseline and to stroke side of hitter	Aim for the baseline in throwing the ball through the volley line
Retriever **#1**	Baseline behind tosser	Retrieve balls and return to tosser
#2	Baseline behind hitter	Retrieve balls and return to tosser
#3	Baseline opposite #1	Retrieve balls and return to tosser

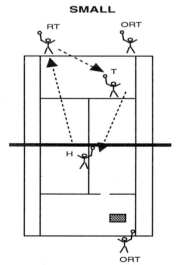

Figure 7.3 *Volley, small group*

VOLLEYS (6-10 PLAYERS PER COURT)

For larger groups, divide the court lengthwise. Assign a group of 3-5 players to each half of the court and proceed with the drills as explained for smaller groups (Figure 7.4).

LARGE

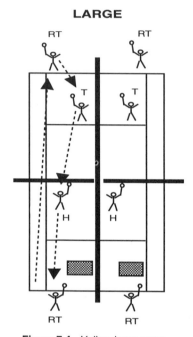

Figure 7.4 *Volley, large group*

ONE ON ONE/ TWO ON ONE DRILLS

These drills are for intermediate or advanced players who have the ability to control the direction of the bal.l Most of the strokes can be incorporated into these drills.   Important reminders for these drills are:

1. The first ball sets the rhythm for the remainder of the rally.
2. Keep the ball in play. Stress control rather than power.
3. Concentrate on each stroke.

A one on one workout is illustrated below (Figures 7.5-7.8). Each part of the total drill should be done for 3-5 minutes. each.

CROSS COURT

forehand--backhand   backhand--forehand

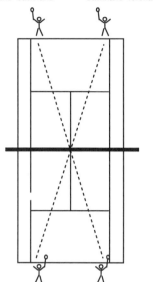

Figure 7.5 *Groundstrokes, cross court (one on one)*

DOWN THE LINE

forehands & backhands

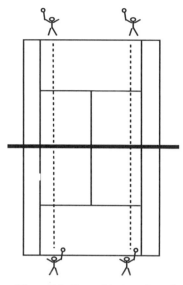

Figure 7.6 *Groundstrokes, down the line (one on one)*

CROSS COURT

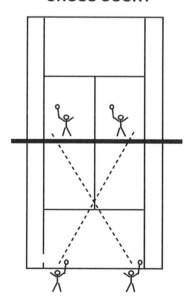

Figure 7.7 *Volley, cross court (one on one)*

DOWN THE LINE

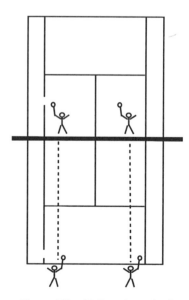

Figure 7.8 *Volley, down the line (one on one)*

A two-on-one workout is a much faster paced drill. The lone player on one side of the net will play the baseline position and hit groundstrokes for the first half of the drill (Figure 7.9). During the second half of the drill, this player will play the net position and hit volleys to the two players at the baseline (Figure 7.10). The lone player must work hard to keep the ball in play. The two players working together on the same side of the net must concentrate on challenging the lone player and not try for "winners".

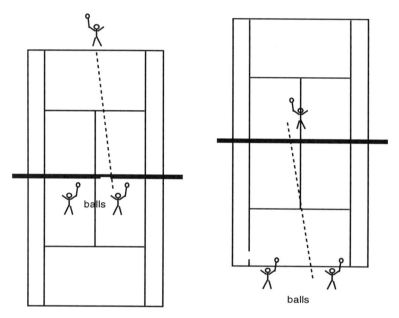

Figure 7.9 *Groundstrokes (two on one)*

Figure 7.10 *Volley (two on one)*

SERVE AND RETURN

The server and returner positions are illustrated in Figure 7.11. The positions and responsibilities of each are described below.

	POSITION	RESPONSIBILITY
Server	Behind baseline between center line and singles sideline	Hit ball to service court at a diagonal
Returner	Behind baseline between center line and singles sideline	Hit the ball cross court

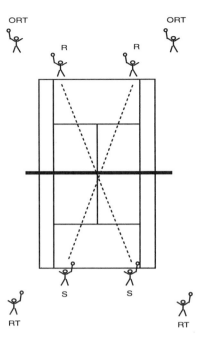

Figure 7.11 *Serve and return*

If more than two people occupy a court, people may be rotated in from retriever position behind server #3 and behind returner #4. Rotation is in a clockwise manner.

SERVE AND VOLLEY

The beginning positions and responsibilities are the same as for the serve and return. The deuce and ad sides alternate hitting. The purpose of this drill is to play the point out crosscourt.

The sequence of the drill calls for the server to serve the ball into the proper court, then move into a position around the service line where a half-volley/approach shot is hit, and then to advance to the net for a volley (Figure 7.12).

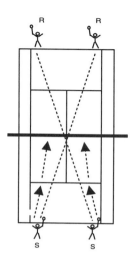

Figure 7.12 *Serve and volley*

RACQUET CONTROL DRILLS
FOR PARTNERS

Each player is positioned on the service line. The objective of this drill is a volley to volley sequence attempting to keep the ball in the air. Forehand and backhand volleys may be practiced. A variation of this drill is to use the half-volley. In this case, the ball must bounce in the service square.

CROSS COURT   **DOWN THE LINE**

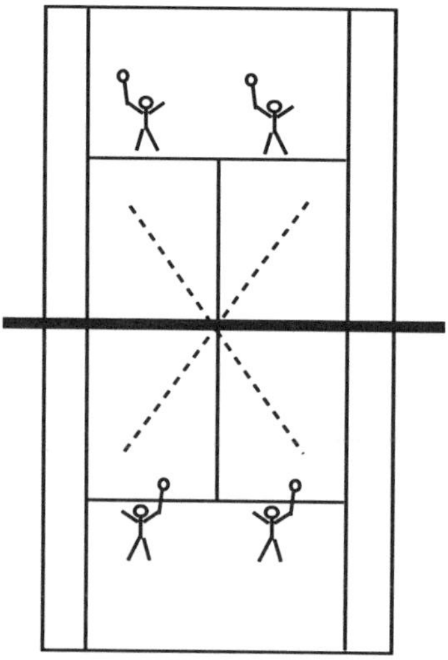

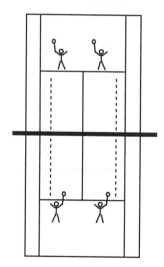

Figure 7.13 *Racquet control drills for partners, cross court*

Figure 7.14 *Racquet control drills for partners, down the line*

RACQUET CONTROL DRILLS FOR 4 PEOPLE

The same drill can be adapted for four people. The hitting pattern is illustrated in Figure 7.15.

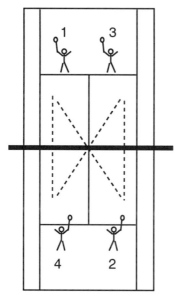

Figure 7.15 *Racquet control drills for 4 people*

RACQUET GAMES

Racquet games are good motivational activities as well as providing for a change of pace. The games which are described can be played with as little as 2 players or as many 10.

GAME OF 21 (ONE ON ONE)

Purpose: Practice hitting groundstrokes deep (Figure 7.16).

Rules: 1)   Bounce hit to begin, either player from behind baseline
    2)   Ball must land between service and baselines, and within singles sidelines
    3)   Set and return are not counted as winners or errors
    4)   Point awarded to opponent of player unable to return ball to designated area (see Rule 2)

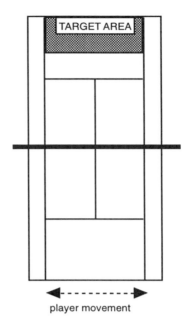

player movement

Figure 7.16 *Game of 21*

GAME OF 15 (ONE ON ONE)

Purpose: Practice passing shots and volleys (Figure 7.17 A-D).

Rules: 1)   Begin with one player behind baseline and
                one player between service line and net
          2)   Bounce hit to begin, either player
          3)   Ball must land in one-half court width-wise*
                (Baseline to net and center line to singles
                sideline)
          4)   Set and return not counted as winners or
                errors
          5)   Point awarded to opponent of player unable
                to return ball to designated area (see Rule
                #3)
*The court boundaries can be altered to practice different shot
angles.

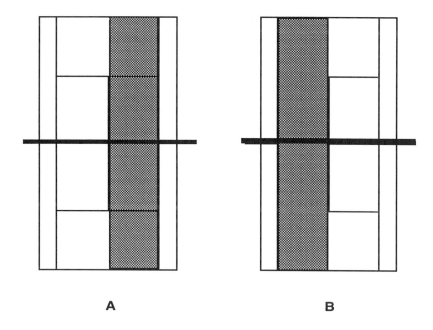

A   B

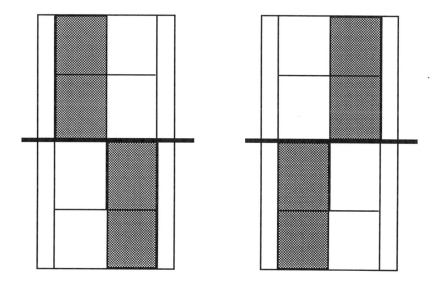

C   D

Figure 7.17 *Boundary variations*

SERVE AND VOLLEY (ONE ON ONE)

Purpose: Practice serve and volley (Figure 7.18).

Rules: 1)   Each serves 5 points from the deuce court
                and 5 points from the ad court
           2)   A point is scored when the ball is not re-
                turned to the designated court area

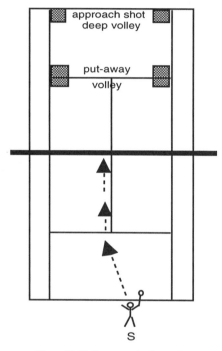

Figure 7.18 *Serve and volley points*

MINI-COURT SINGLES OR DOUBLES (2-4 PLAYERS)

Purpose: Racquet control

Rules: 1)   Same scoring and rotation as full court game
           2)   Serve is a bounce hit, 2 chances per point
           3)   Boundaries are the service courts only
           4)   Volleys are legal but not advised unless
                these are skilled players

RECORD SETTERS (2-4 PLAYERS)

Purpose: Racquet control, concentration, competition

Rules:
1) Volleys—count how many consecutive volleys 2(4) players can hit across the net without letting the ball bounce.
2) 1/2 volleys—Count how many consecutive times 2(4) players can hit ball across net landing in service court(s) with one bounce

AROUND THE WORLD (2-MANY)

Purpose: Practice groundstrokes and volleys, group activity, racquet control, conditioning, concentration (Figure 7.19).

Rules:
1) Divide group in 1/2, placing 1/2 at one baseline (service line), and the other 1/2 across the net at the other baseline (service line)
2) Move group out of racquet range (3-6') of first player in line
3) First player in line drops and hits ball over net to player in opposite line
4) After hitting ball, player runs clockwise around court to end of opposite line
5) Two errors by one player eliminates that player from further competition (set does not count)
6) When only 2 players remain, players no longer run around court. They rally until one player is eliminated by error.

Safety Notes:
1) All players must rotate in the same direction
2) To avoid getting hit, keep line back against fence (baseline for volleys), except for the person hitting

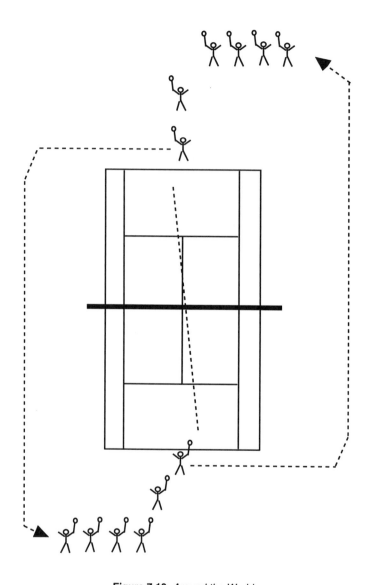

Figure 7.19 *Around the World*

Chapter 8

STRATEGY: GAME SITUATIONS

The game of tennis is won by forcing your opponent into making errors or by placing the ball where your opponent cannot reach it. Strategy is a plan of attack for placing your opponent in some sort of disadvantageous position. In keeping with the theme of the book, this chapter will emphasize the basics of strategy.

SINGLES STRATEGY

THE GROUNDSTROKE OR BASELINE GAME

Several of the more notable tennis professionalswho use the groundstroke or baseline game are Steffi Graf, Arantxa Sanchez Vicario, Mary Pierce, Jim Courier, Michael Chang, and Andre Agassi. They base their strategy on *consistency* thereby, allowing their opponents to commit the errors. This type of game is best suited for slower court surfaces such as clay.

The objectives of the groundstroke or baseline game are:

1. Move your opponent around. Keep them guessing where the next shot will be.
2. Keep the ball clearance over the net at about 3-6 feet to ensure depth of ball placement to your opponent's court. Also, this provides a reduced margin for your own forced errors.
3. Be patient. You may need to hit many (20 or more) shots to win one point.

ALL-COURT GAME

This is the most versatile of strategies. It simply means that the player uses the baseline and the net for an assortment of shots. This game is best suited to hard court surfaces. Examples of tennis professionals who have an all-court game are Jimmy Connors, MaliVai Washington, Zina Garrison-Jackson, Jana Novotna, Yevgeny Kafelnikov, and Chanda Rubin.

The basic objectives of this type of play are:

1. Keep the opponent off balance by using a variety of shots from both the baseline and the net.
2. Use a groundstroke game until the opponent hits a short ball allowing for a more aggressive approach and volley game.

SERVE AND VOLLEY GAME

A serve and volley game is the ultimate in aggressive strategies. The object is to approach the net immediately after serving. Several tennis professionals who use this style of play are Pete Sampras, Michael Stich, Stefan Edberg, Martina Navritolova, and Helena Sukova. Most important to the success of this strategy is the quality (power and placement) of the first serve. The object is to serve well enough to elicit a weak return of serve.

The second critical shot is the approach shot which will be either a half-volley or volley. This shot is most often hit around the service line after a split-step in "no man's land". The mythical "no man's land" cannot be avoided when approaching the net. You should practice shots between the service line and "no man's land" because the quality of the shot hit in this area dictates volley opportunities. One caution, do not remain in the approach area ("no man's land") but continue toward the net once the approach has been hit.

Another important point in approaching the net is control and balance. When the ball is hit by the opponent, the direction of the ball is changed. Therefore, a change of direction is required by the server approaching the net. The most efficient way to change directions is to be balanced over the balls of your feet with the body square to (facing) the net. To achieve this position when running to the net, a split-step is used. That is a slight jump landing on the balls of both feet creating an unweighted ready position. From this position, an immediate change of direction can be achieved. With a serve and volley game, the opponent is pressured into returning the ball before he/she is ready. When the server reaches the net, the opponent is forced into making very carefully placed shots (passing shot) to avoid hitting the ball to the server. This strategy is suited best for grass or fast, hard courts.

The objectives of this type of game are:

1. Make the first serve a deep and powerful one.
2. Use a split-step prior to hitting an approach shot deep into your opponent's court.
3. Close in toward the net to angle the volley away from your opponent for a winner.

DOUBLES STRATEGY

ONE UP, ONE BACK

The one up, one back strategy occurs when one partner plays the net position while the other partner plays the baseline position (Figure 8.1). This game is suited for those who are fond of hitting groundstrokes, and are insecure about their volleys. However, there is a major gap between partners. This is especially apparent if the ball is hit to the opposing net person (Figure 8.2). In the one up, one back strategy, it is important for the net person to keep moving with and watching the ball at all times.

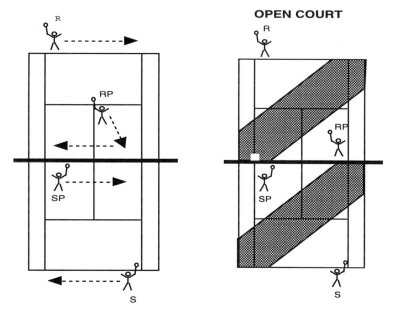

Figure 8.1 *One up, one back*   **Figure 8.2** *One up, one back*

TWO UP

This is by far the most aggressive type of doubles play, and is predicated on the serve and volley. Generally, the first team to the net wins. The position of both players obviously is at the net (Figure 8.3). With both players side by side and close to the net, the opponents are left with very little room to hit a safe shot. However, this type of strategy does leave the team vulnerable to the lob (Figure 8.4).

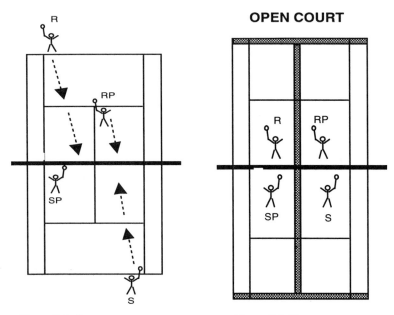

OPEN COURT

Figure 8.3 *Two up*   **Figure 8.4** *Two up*

The keys to this game are:

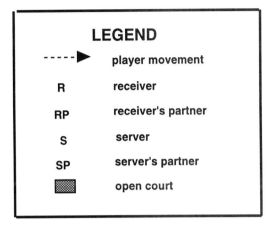

LEGEND

- - - - - ▶ player movement

R receiver

RP receiver's partner

S server

SP server's partner

▨ open court

1. Follow the ball as a team.
2. Move in the direction of the moving ball.
3. Split step as the ball is being hit.
4. Never take your eyes off the ball. The exeception to this is when your partner is serving.
5. Always assume the next shot will be yours.

TWO BACK

Both partners in the two back position play along the baseline (Figure 8.5). This is the ultimate in *defensive* games. It is used only if your opponent has an excellent serve. A powerful, well placed serve makes the return of serve more difficult. .A weak return allows the server's net partner an opportunity at an offensive "put away". In this situation, the returner's net partner has very little time react to the offensive volley of the opponent. To contend with this situation, the "two back" strategy for the return of serve can be employed. This strategy allows for opponents to use the forecourt (with shots such as angle volleys) for winners (Figure 8.6).

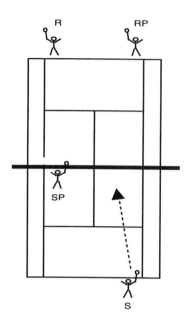

Figure 8.5 *Two back*

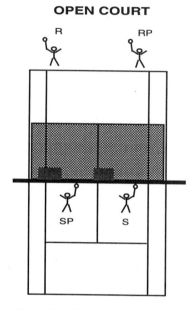

Figure 8.6 *Two back*

Chapter 9

FACILITIES, SURFACES, EQUIPMENT

Whether new designs in facilities, surfaces, and equipment caused an increased interest in the game of tennis, or whether the growth in popularity of the sport demanded these things is like asking "Which came first—the chicken or the egg?" In any case, there are a variety of facilities and surfaces available for players to use and a number of choices in equipment to meet individual needs. All of these have made the game easier to learn and more enjoyable to play.

Recreational tennis

FACILITIES

Facilities range from free public courts to privately owned clubs which charge a membership fee. Everyone who desires to play the game of tennis should have access to a facility. The following are examples of such facilities.

---

1. Open public courts. These are free to the public and are found at school grounds or small parks.
2. Organized public courts. This usually includes a minimal fee for use.
3. Indoor racquet clubs. Indoor courts normally involve an initial fee for membership followed by monthly fees and court time fees.
4. Outdoor racquet clubs. Outdoor racquet clubs have similar expenses as indoor racquet clubs, but are not quite as expensive.
5. Country clubs. These are privately owned facilities, usually golf oriented with tennis as an adjunct sport. Membership fees are required.

SURFACES

There are four basic types of surfaces: hard (concrete or asphalt), clay, grass, and synthetic. The advantages and disadvantages of each are provided in Table 9.1.

The hard and synthetic courts are best suited for the player with an all-around game. Ball bounces are quite reliable on these surfaces. Grass courts, on the other hand, favor the serve and volley player because the ball bounces are fast, low, and unpredictable. Clay courts favor the baseline player because the ball bounces are slow and high. For the obvious reason of maintenance costs, the hard courts are by far the most popular court in existence in the United States.

Surface	Advantage	Disadvantage
hard	inexpensive maintainenance free dries fast	legs tire quickly collects dust, dirt, sand
clay	good in damp climate good shock absorption	high maintenance
grass	less fatiguing on legs cool surface	high maintenance slippery when wet
synthetic	low maintenance durable transportable excellent traction good drainage	expensive

Table 9.1   *Advantages and Disadvantages of Various Surface Types*

EQUIPMENT

The major pieces of equipment discussed in this section will be the racquet, the ball, and the shoes. These have undergone much scientific development since they were first used in the early days of tennis.

Equipment selection

RACQUETS

The selection of a racquet for a tennis player is becoming almost as complicated as the selection of a shoe for a runner. At one time there were few options available in choosing a racquet. They were made of wood and were of a standard size. The only options left open to the player were the weight of the racquet, grip size, and string tension. Today, the options have become much more difficult because "science" has entered into the development and construction of the racquet. Research design emphasis has been placed on racquet composition, weight, stiffness, string tension, and overall size. All of this has been in the interest of making the racquet individualized. That is, a racquet can more nearly meet the individual needs of the player, such as body size, skill level, and style of play.

Several questions should be posed before selecting a racquet. How much do I wish to spend on a racquet? (Racquets range in price from $30 to $500). How long will I need to use this racquet before purchasing a new one? Do I have any limiting injuries such as tennis elbow? What type of body stature do I have? What skill level do I possess? Knowing this information will assist in making a correct selection of a racquet based on its size, weight, composition, stiffness, grip size, strings, and string tension.

Composition

Racquet composition may be wood, metal, fiberglass, graphite, boron, ceramic, or a combination of fibers. Generally speaking, the wood racquets are inexpensive, but are rarely used anymore. Th metal racquets last longer and are inexpensive. Fiberglass racquets are light weight, but not durable. Graphite racquets are durable and expensive, but has the advantage of less vibration. Recent racquet technology has produced the wide body racquet. It has a thicker, more aerodynamic frame, and is made with a combination of materials.

Sizes

The three major categories of racquets are standard (70 sq. in.), mid-size (85-95 sq. in.), and oversize (100+ sq. in.). ITF (International Tennis Federation), of which the USTA is a member, has specified the maximum size of the racquet. The advantage of the larger racquets is in the effective area, or larger "sweet spot". In implements which are used for striking objects, there is an area designated as the "sweet spot" or "center of percussion". In the instance of a tennis racquet the "sweet spot" is an area where the ball may hit and not cause a twisting action or a vibratory action in the hands. When a ball is hit away from the "sweet spot", the vibrations can be felt in the hands. The larger racquets have larger "sweet spots" which increases the effective hitting area. Balls which may have been hit off-center on the smaller racquets will cause the ball to be miss-hit, whereas on the larger racquets, these hits will be good.

Weight

Racquets vary in weight from 10 to 15 ounces. Lightweight racquets generally are used by players of small stature, or by players who like to work the racquet. The heavier racquets are used by players of larger stature, or by those who want the weight to provide power. The key is in finding a racquet that feels comfortable for you.

Grip Size

Grip size is an individual matter. The racquet should feel comfortable, and should be non-fatiguing. A suggested guide for selection is as follows:

4 - 4 3/8	small hands
4 1/2	medium size hands
4 5/8 - 5	large hands

Stiffness vs. Flexibility

A racquet is considered to be stiff or flexible depending on its composition and shape. Stiffer racquets provide for better control. However, a very stiff racquet may cause more vibration. Players with arm and elbow problems may wish to avoid the very stiff racquet. Scientific testing provides the initial information as to weight and stiffness. Individual testing, however, is still the most important factor in choosing a new racquet.

Strings

Strings are made of either gut or synthetic material. Gut strings are the usual choice of professionals, but they cost more and do not last as long as the synthetic strings. Synthetic strings perform quite effectively and are the preferred choice of non-professionals.

String Tension

String tension varies from 40 to 80 lbs. The tighter the tension, up to a point, the more control you have. Lower tensions have been shown to produce greater ball velocities after impact. Somewhere in between the two tension extremes should provide the best combination for power and control. When in doubt, consult the manufacturer's recommended string tension guidelines. Remember that proper string tension is the final determining factor as to the comfort of a racquet.

BALLS

The old traditional white-colored ball is no longer used. The official ball for all tournament play is yellow. The primary reason for the change was an advantage in being able to see the ball better. No matter the color, it must be of a uniform size (2 1/2 " to 2 5/8") and of a uniform weight (2 to 2 1/16 oz.). When dropped on concrete at a height of 100 inches, it must have the ability to rebound to a height of between 53 inches and 58 inches.

The type of ball used depends on the surface being used. A ball with a regular nap is best for softer courts. Extra duty nap is recommended for all American hard courts.

Pressurized and non-pressurized balls are available. Basically, the non-pressurized balls are used in high altitudes.

TENNIS SHOES

For years, runners had the luxury of selecting shoes from hundreds of scientifically designed models on the market. The same was not true for tennis players who basically settled for a "generic" shoe for play. This situation changed in recent years, and shoes made for specific foot types and surface types are now on the market.

Tennis shoe selection

Recent research in shoe design has shown the importance of knowing how the foot moves on the court. By observing the movement patterns in slow motion via a high speed motion picture camera, a shoe designer can note where the foot stresses are likely to occur. Furthermore, the designer can note the differences in movement patterns on different court surfaces.

Another research technique which has been used to further research foot movement patterns on the court is force plate analysis. By stepping on a pressure-sensitive plate, the researcher can tell where the major pressure areas are on the foot during various phases of the movement.

What has research shown us? The following shoe features are the result of shoe design research, and are considered to be desirable in selecting a good shoe for your foot.

1. Traction. We know that the game of tennis involves a great deal of lateral movement. Shoe designers have given the sole design some careful thought in this regard. The design of the sole enables the player to stop quickly and immediately change directions. The various designs (e.g. wavy, circular) allow the player to do precisely this without sliding or stopping abruptly.

2. Forefoot and rearfoot stability. In moving laterally or forward and backward, the foot must be stabilized. A shoe which shows good support, such as strapping, in the forefoot area and rearfoot area will prevent the foot from "sliding" off the bottom of the shoe.

3. Cushioning. We know that the foot strikes the ground many times during the game, and each time it does it experiences a weight (force) on it several times the body weight. Therefore, the shoe needs to have cushioning ability in the heel and forefoot area.

4. Flexibility. The foot movement involves much   bending and extending at the toes. For this reason, a shoe should be "flexible". If you were to pick up a shoe and hold it under the heel with one hand, under the toe with the other, and then bend it in the center, you would discover how flexible that shoe was.

5. Toe box reinforcement. Tennis players tend to scrape or drag the toes on the ground. This is particularly true of some servers. A shoe with a reinforced toe box would be desirable in these cases.

The major question narrows down to "What shoe should I buy?" Assuming you have considered all of the important shoe features mentioned previously, consider the shape of your foot. This may provide us with a general guideline for buying a shoe which will be functional for you. In fact, most shoe guides now base their descriptions and suggested shoes based on foot type.

Look at the shape of your foot. Do you have a low arch (a pes planus foot)? This foot shape tends to roll over toward the inner border of the foot very easily, thereby placing stress on the inside of the ankle or knee. This foot would benefit from a shoe which has good support in the arch. Do you have a high arch (a cavus or rigid foot)? This foot type finds it difficult to roll toward the inner border, but rather tends to stay on the outer borders of the foot. This foot type would benefit from a more flexible arch support. Do you have a "normal" arch (a rectus foot)? You are in good shape!

Now look at the sole of the tennis shoe. Notice its shape. This is called a last. It is the form around which the shoe is built. Notice if the shoe has a straight last or a curved last (Figures 9.1 and 9.2). If you have a high arch, the shoe with the curved last probably would be best for you. This type of shoe lacks support material in the arch area, and would allow the foot to roll over toward its inner border. The flat arched foot, on the other hand, needs a shoe with more support material to prevent excessive rolling to the inside. The straight last has more support material in the arch region. The normal foot probably would be comfortable in a slightly curved last. Remember this is a suggested general guideline. Players with special foot problems should consult a podiatrist for further evaluation.

Figure 9.1 *Straight lasted shoe*

Figure 9.2 *Slightly curved lasted shoe*

Chapter 10

THINKING WITH THE EYES

Contributed by: Nancy Dunavant King, Ph.D.

"Thinking with the eyes" is a phrase that describes how a person learns, then improves a skill. The first step in this process is to create a visual picture of the movement in the brain. This cognitive process is achieved when a teacher demonstrates the proper technique. That image is encoded into the brain with all the senses: the eyes transmit the image and that image imprints on the mind, the ears provide an auditory cue as well as kinesthetic or balance cues that accompanies the image, and the nervous system stimulates muscles required ot perform the movement being demonstrated by the teacher. All of this takes a split second, and if encoded properly, and stored in our memory, learning takes place. In addition to encoding procedures that must take place, learning is enhanced when there is an emotional component to learning a skill (i.e., being motivated to learn). Wanting to learn a skill strengthens all of the processes mentioned above, and if a person is motivated, quickens the learning process.

Learning styles is another way in which the learning process is understood. When learning, some people may be "visual" learners in that their learning takes place when visual cues are presented, when they can use their sight as their primary learning source. "Auditory" learners learn best when they can hear what is being taught. A "kinesthetic" learner uses the sense of touch to learn. Maximal learning takes place when all of these preferences, visual, auditory, kinesthetic, or tactile are integrated in the learning process.

In addition to learning that takes place on the court, learning can also take place off the court. "Thinking with one's eyes" off the court involves creating a mental picture, or visualizing the skill that that is being learned. In fact, visualizing is a form of rehearsal that takes place within the realm of the mind/body connection and can be executed anywhere at any time. Creating a perfect mental picture of how the skill is performed creates a physiological response that innervates muscles and neurons used in the execution of the skill being visualized. It is very important that a perfect picture be visualized even though perfect execution of the skill itself is very difficult, if not impossible.

In order for visualization to be most effective, it is important that the body be in a relaxed state. Breathing deeply three or four times, or contracting then relaxing specific muscle groups, are quick and effective methods that can also be done anywhere, any time and, with practice takes only 5-10 mintues to prepare the mind to visualize the skills learned on the court. Houston, the author of the book *The Possible Human*, wrote that we now have confirmed what the mind vividly experiences can increase heart rate, blood flow, skin temperature, affect brain waves (i.e., the entire body).

In their study of elite athletes competing in the 1984 Olympics, Porter and Foster (1986) found that Olympic athletes visualized their performances weeks or months prior to competition, a factor that was not as prevalent among non-elite athletes. The integration of what the mind thinks and how the body reacts empowers an individual to believe that he/she has control, on and off the court, over how well a skill is learned and how effortlessly it can be performed.

Visualization can also be applied to how we perceive our environment and how we feel about that environment. In other words, emotions can be visualized. Creating a mental picture of a tennis serve will be most successful if a perfect serve is visualized AND accompanied by a feeling of confidence. Positive or negative emotions complement visualization of a skill, which in turn complements the physical execution of the skill. Performance is only as good as the weakest link in this process.

Listed below is an example of the steps used to visualize a skill in tennis:

- Begin by taking 3-4 deep breaths or muscle contraction/release to relax.

- See in your mind's eye the whole process, or the complete picture as though you were watching yourself from a distance.

- Be aware of the environment, the court, others around you, aware with all of your senses, smelling the air, feeling the temperatures.

- Picture yourself walking onto the court, preparing to warm up, stretching, talking with others, relaxing.

- Feel yourself being confident, excited, in control of your body.

- Take deep breaths if you begin to feel nervous or anxious.

- Visualize performing a particular skill, or playing an entire game, perfectly.

- Accompany each skill performed with positive emotions such as satisfaction, pleasure, exhilaration.

- Visualize completion of the skill(s), feeling satisfied and confident.

- See yourself moving off the court, warming down, and feeling a sense of accomplishment.

Creating perfect mental pictures with the appropriate emotional response is a skill that must be practiced if it is to be learned. Good visualization does not just happen just as excellent tennis serves or strokes do not just happen. The more the mental and physical skills are practiced in conjunction with one another, the quicker a person will learn and be able to play a complete game of tennis. People who rehearse physically and mentally have the edge over those who only practice one way or the other.

Gallwey (1976) recommended that two entities are always at work: the mind and the body. These two entities can work together, or antagonistically. Rehearsal on and off the court together. If a player thinks about tennis only when he/she is on the court, then learning the skill will take longer than if he/she also thinks about it while off the court. Thinking with eyes and feeling the body play tennis further strengthens the link between mind and body, or as a famous comedian once said, "What you see is what you get".

References

Gallwey, W.T. (1976) *Inner Tennis*. New York: Random House.

Houston, J. (1982). *The Possible Human*. Los Angeles: J.P. Tarcher.

Porter, K. and Foster, J. (19486) *The Mental Athlete*. New York: Ballatine Books.

SUMMARIZED RULES OF TENNIS

**Reprinted by permission of
United States Tennis Association**

INTRODUCTION

The official rules of tennis are summarized below for the convenience of all players. In the preparation of this summary, no changes were made in the official rules, which have been established by the International Tennis Federation and are adhered to by the United States Tennis Association. Some technical aspects, however, such as specifications on court size and equipment, balls and rackets, have been deleted here for the sake of brevity. For those who are interested in these specifications, they are covered in their entirety in the complete *Rules of Tennis*, which also includes interpretative Cases and Decisions and USTA Comments.

Another invaluable reference for players is *The Code,* whose principles and guidelines apply to unofficiated matches. Players all over the world follow not only the official rules of tennis but also the traditions of sportsmanship and fair play found in *The Code.*

A familiarity with these rules and traditions is essential for achieving the greatest possible benefit and enjoyment from tennis. Information on how to purchase the *Rules of Tennis* and *The Code* may be found on the inside back cover.

THE SINGLES GAME

SERVER AND RECEIVER

The players stand on opposite sides of the net; the player who first delivers the ball is called the Server and the other, the Receiver.

DIAGRAM OF COURT

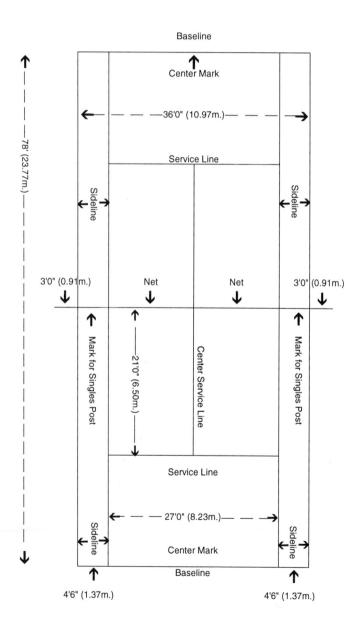

CHOICE OF SIDES AND SERVICE

The choice of sides and the right to be Server or Receiver in the first game is decided by toss. The player winning the toss may choose or require his opponent to choose: (a) the right to be Server or Receiver, in which case the other player shall choose the side; or (b) the side, in which case the other player shall choose the right to be Server or Receiver.

DELIVERY OF SERVICE

The service is delivered in the following manner: immediately before commencing to serve, the Server positions himself with both feet at rest behind the baseline and within the imaginary continuation of the center mark and the sideline of the singles court. He shall not serve until the Receiver is ready.

The server then throws the ball into the air in any direction and strikes it with his racket before it hits the ground. Delivery is deemed complete at the moment the racket strikes the ball.

RETURN OF SERVICE

The Receiver may stand wherever he pleases on his own side of the net. However, he must allow the ball to hit the ground before returning the service. If the Receiver attempts to return the service, he shall be deemed ready.

SERVICE FROM ALTERNATE COURTS

In delivering the service, the Server stands alternately behind the right and left courts, beginning from the right in every game. The ball served shall pass over the net and hit the ground within the service court which is diagonally opposite, or upon any line bounding such court, before the Receiver returns it.

If the ball is erroneously served from the wrong half of the court, the resulting play stands, but service from the proper court, in accordance with the score, shall be resumed immediately after this discovery.

FAULTS

The service is a fault if the Server misses the ball in attempting to serve it, if the ball does not land in the proper service court, or if the ball served touches a permanent fixture other than the net, strap or band before it hits the ground.

Throughout the delivery of the service, the Server shall keep both feet behind the baseline and shall not change his position by walking or running. A foot fault is called when the Server steps on the baseline or into the court before his racket meets the ball.

SERVICE AFTER A FAULT

After a first fault, the Server serves again from behind the same half of the court from which he served that fault (unless it was a fault because he served from behind the wrong half, in which case he is entitled to deliver one service from behind the proper half).

A SERVICE LET

During the service, a ball that touches the net but lands in the proper court is termed a "let" and counts for nothing. That one service is replayed. There is no limit to the number of let balls that may be made on the service; the Server continues serving into the same court until a good service is delivered or two faults are made.

RECEIVER BECOMES SERVER

At the end of the first game, the Receiver becomes Server and the Server, Receiver; and so on alternately in all the   subsequent games of a match. The players change sides at the end of the first, third and every subsequent alternate game.

If a player serves out of turn, the player who ought to have served shall serve as soon as the mistake is discovered. All points scored before such discovery shall stand. If a game has been completed before such discovery, the order of service remains as altered.

SERVER WINS POINT

The Server wins the point if the ball served, not being a let, touches the Receiver or anything which he wears or carries before it hits the ground or if the receiver otherwise loses the point as described below.

RECEIVER WINS POINT

The Receiver wins the point if the Server serves two consecutive faults or otherwise loses the point as described below.

BALL FALLING ON LINE - GOOD

A ball falling on a line is regarded as falling in the court bounded by that line.

PLAYER LOSES POINT

A player loses the point if:
(a) he fails to return the ball in play directly over or past the end of the net before it has hit the ground twice consecutively; or
(b) he returns the ball in play so that it hits the ground, a permanent fixture (other than the net, posts or singles sticks, cord or metal cable strap or band), or other object outside any of the lines which bound his opponent's court; or
(c) he deliberately carries or catches the ball in play on his racket or deliberately touches it with his racket more than once; or
(d) he or his racket touches the net, post or the ground within his opponent's court at any time while the ball is in play; or
(e) he volleys the ball before it has passed the net; or
(f) he volleys the ball and fails to make a good return even when standing outside the court; or
(g) the throws his racket at and hits the ball; or
(h) he deliberately and materially changes the shape of his racket during the playing of the point; or
(i) he deliberately commits any act which hinders his opponent in making a stroke; or
(j) the ball in play touches him or anything that he wears or carries other than the racket in his hand

A GOOD RETURN

It is a good return if:

(a)   the ball touches and passes over the net, posts, cord or metal cable, strap or band and hits the ground within the court; or

(b)   the ball touches any other permanent fixture after it has hit the ground within the proper court; or

(c)   the ball hits the ground within the proper court and rebounds back over the net and the player whose turn it is to strike reaches over the net and plays the ball, provided that neither he nor any part of his clothes or racket touches the net, and that the stroke is otherwise good; or

(d)   the ball is returned from outside the post, provided that it hits the ground within the proper court; or

(e)   a player's racket passes over the net after he has properly returned the ball; or

(f)   a player succeeds in returning the ball which has struck another ball lying in the court.

A LET

In all cases where a let (other than a service let) has to be called under the rules or to provide for an interruption of play, the point shall be replayed.

If a player is hindered in making a stroke by anything not within his control, except a permanent fixture or deliberate interference by his opponent, a let shall be called.

COACHING

A player may not receive coaching during the playing of any match other than one that is part of a team competition.

THE DOUBLES GAME

The above Rules apply to the Doubles Game except as below.

DELIVERY OF SERVICE

The Server positions himself with both feet at rest behind the baseline and within the imaginary continuation of the center mark and the sideline of the doubles court.

ORDER OF SERVICE

At the beginning of each set, the pair serving the first game decides which partner shall do so and the opposing pair decides similarly for the second game. The partner of the player who served in the first game serves in the third; the partner of the player who served in the second game serves in the fourth, and so on in the same order in all subsequent games of a set.

ORDER OF RECEIVING

The pair receiving the service in the first game of each set decides which partner shall receive in the right-hand court, and the opposing pair decides similarly in the second game of each set. Partners receive the service alternately throughout each game. The order of receiving the service shall not be altered during the set but may be changed at the beginning of a new set.

SERVICE OUT OF TURN

If a partner serves out of his turn, the partner who ought to have served shall serve as soon as the mistake is discovered, but all points scored and any faults served before such discovery shall stand. If a game has been completed before such discovery, the order of service remains as altered.

RECEIVING OUT OF TURN

If during a game the order of receiving the service is changed by the Receivers, it remains as altered until the end of the game, but the partners shall resume their original order of receiving in the next game of that set in which they are the Receivers.

SERVED BALL TOUCHING PLAYER

The service is a fault if the ball touches the Server's partner or anything which he wears or carries. The Server wins the point if the ball served (not being a let) touches the partner of the Receiver, or anything he wears or carries, before it hits the ground.

BALL STRUCK ALTERNATELY

The ball shall be struck by one or the other player of the opposing pairs in the course of making a service or a return. If both of them hit the ball, either simultaneously or consecutively, their opponents win the point.

SCORING

A GAME

If a player wins his first point, the score is called 15 for that player; on winning his second point, his score is called 30, on winning his third point, his score is called 40; and the fourth point won by a player is scored a Game for that player except as follows:
If both players have won three points, the score is called Deuce; the next point won by a player is scored Advantage for that player. If the same player wins the next point, he wins the Game. If the other player wins the next point, the score is again called Deuce; and so on, until a player wins the two points immediately following the score at Deuce, when the Game is scored for that player.

A SET

A player (or players) who first wins six games wins a Set, except that he must win by a margin of two games over his opponent. Where necessary, a Set is extended until this margin is achieved (unless a tie-break system of scoring has been announced in advance of the match).
The players change sides at the end of the first, third, and every subsequent alternate game of each set and at the end of

each set unless the total number of games in such set is even, in which case the change is not made until the end of the first game of the next set.

The maximum number of sets in a match is five for men and three for women.

THE TIE-BREAK GAME

If announced in advance of the match, a Tie-break Game operates when the score reaches six games all in any set.

In singles, a player who first wins seven points wins the game and the set provided he leads by a margin of two points. If the score reaches six points all the game is extended until this margin has been achieved. Numerical scoring is used throughout the Tie-break Game. The player whose turn it is to serve is the Server for the first point; his opponent is the Server for the second and third points; and, thereafter, each player serves alternately for two consecutive points until the winner of the game and set has been decided.

In doubles, the player whose turn it is to serve is the Server for the first point. Thereafter, each player serves in rotation for two points, in the same order as determined previously in that set, until the winners of the game and set have been decided.

From the first point, each service is delivered alternately from the right and left courts, beginning from the right court. The first Server serves the first point from the right court; the second Server serves the second and third points from the left and right courts, respectively; the next Server serves the fourth and fifth points from the left and right courts, respectively; and so on.

Players change ends after every six points and at the conclusion of the Tie-break Game. The player (or doubles pair) who served first in the Tie-break Game shall receive service in the first game of the following set.

RULES OF WHEELCHAIR TENNIS

The game of wheelchair tennis follows the same rules as able-bodied tennis as endorsed by the International Tennis Federation except the wheelchair tennis player is allowed two bounces of the ball.

"Reprinted with the permission of the United States Tennis Association. For a complete version of the Rules, the Rules of Tennis and Cases and Decisions *may be purchased from the USTA Publications Department, USTA, Inc. 70 West Red Oak Lane, White Plains, NY 10604-3602."*

THE UNWRITTEN RULES OF TENNIS

The written rules of tennis are for the umpire and govern the scoring. The unwritten rules keep the game under control, and refer to a player's conduct on the court. Some of the basic rules of etiquette are:

1. Before you begin play, greet your opponent and introduce yourself.
2. Spin your racquet for choice of serve and side.
3. Check the net height at the center of the court.
4. Be sure your opponent is ready to receive your serve.
5. Announce a set score before starting a new game and the game score prior to serving each point.
6. Foot faults are called when officials are on the court. They usually are not called when officials are not

Unwritten rules

present.

7. During rallies, call all shots made on your side of the net. If a ball is "out", call it immediately and refrain from making a play on it.

8. If there is doubt as to whether the ball is in or out, play it as "in".

9. Wait until play is completed on an adjacent court when your ball has rolled over there.

10. If a ball from another court rolls onto your court, wait to return the ball until the point has been completed on that court.

11. Acknowledge a good play by your opponent.

12. Control your temper at all times.

Appendix **C**

TENNIS TERMINOLOGY

AD–short for advantage (p. 106)

AD IN–advantage of one point in favor of server after a deuce game (p. 107)

AD OUT–advantage of one point in favor of receiver after a deuce game (p. 107)

AEROBICS–activities which involve a continuous pattern of movement such as runing, swimming, cycling, etc. (p. 19)

ALL-COURT GAME–strategy in singles play which combines baseline and net play (p. 83)

APPROACH–a stroke used in advancing toward the net when the opponent's ball has been hit somewhere near the service line; (p. 50)

BACKHAND DRIVE–a groundstroke which is hit from the left side of the body for right-handed players, and from the right side for left-handed players (p. 28)

BASELINE–end boundary line of a tennis court (p. 100)

BASELINE GAME–strategy used in singles play where player hits groundstrokes from the end boundary line (p. 83)

CARDIOVASCULAR ENDURANCE–ability to sustain an activity over an extended period of time (p. 19)

CAVUS FOOT–a high-arched foot (p. 96)

CENTER LINE–the perpendicular line from the net dividing the court into two equal halves or service areas (p. 100)

CENTER OF PERCUSSION–area of tennis racquet where ball contact causes the least amount of vibration; or creates the greatest rebound; also known as the "sweet spot" (p. 92)

CONCENTRIC CONTRACTION–results from an exercise which is performed in the opposite direction as the force of gravity (p. 8)

CONDITIONING–a program of strength and power development, stretching/flexibility, and cardiovascular endurance designed for performing at optimal efficiency (p. 5)

CONTACT PHASE–phase in stroke execution where racquet meets ball (p. 26)

CONTINENTAL GRIP–an alternate method of holding the racquet in which the hand is placed midway between the Eastern forehand and Eastern backhand grip (p. 36)

DAVIS CUP–competition held between men's teams with a nation vs. nation format (p. 2)

DEUCE–a tie game with both players having scored three points (p. 106)

DROP SHOT–a "touch shot" in which the ball is placed in the opponent's forecourt near the net (p. 51)

EASTERN GRIP–hand placement on the racquet used for the groundstrokes and serve (p. 22)

ECCENTRIC CONTRACTION–results from an exercise which is performed in the same direction as the force of gravity (p. 8)

EXERCISE HEART RATE–the rate at which the heart should beat during an aerobic activity; based upon age, maximum heart rate, and desired intensity (p. 19)

FEDERATION CUP–competition held between women's teams with a nation vs. nation format (p. 2)

FLEXIBILITY–the range of motion about a joint (p. 15)

FOLLOW-THROUGH–continuation or finish of a stroke following contact (p. 27)

FOREHAND DRIVE–a groundstroke which is hit from the right side of the body for a right-handed player, and from the left side for a left-handed player (p. 21)

GAME–player who first reaches four points and has a margin of at least two points (p. 106)

GRAND SLAM–a name give for winning the four major tennis championships of Wimbledon, U. S. Open, French Open, and Australian Open (p. 2)

GROUNDSTROKE–either the forehand or backhand drive where the ball bounces one time before being hit (p. 21)

HALF-VOLLEY–a stroke in which contact is made with the ball immediately after it has bounced (p. 50)

INITIAL REACTION–the first movement in response to the oncoming ball p. 25)

LAST–the form over which the upper part of the shoe is pulled during the manufacturing process (p. 96)

LET–a ball that touches the net but lands in the proper court on a serve (p. 102)

LOB–a high arched "touch" shot which can be used as an offensive or defensive shot (p. 48)

MATCH–a maximum of three or five sets for men, and three sets for women (p. 106)

MAXIMUM HEART RATE–an estimate of the highest heart rate which can be achieved in an all-out exercise effort; based on age (p. 19)

NATIONAL RATING SCALE–a classification of individuals according to skill level for the purpose of competition (p. 3)

NO-MAN'S LAND–an imaginary area just behind the service line (p. 84)

ONE UP, ONE BACK–a strategy in doubles play where one partner plays the net position while the other partner plays the baseline position (p. 85)

OVERHEAD–an offensive shot hit from a position above the head and directed downward forcefully into the opponent's court (p. 45)

OVERSPIN—rotation on a ball resutling from it being lifted upward and forward (p. 53)

PASSING SHOT—a ball which is out of the opponent's reach when he/she is at the net (p. 41)

PES PLANUS FOOT—low arched foot (p. 96)

POWER—the rate at which work is done (p. 5)

PREPARATION PHASE—phase in which the racquet is placed in proper position to execute the stroke (p. 21)

RALLY—hitting the ball back and forth across the net (p. 80)

READY POSITION—a balanced and stable position of the body in preparation for reacting to the ball (p. 22)

RECEIVER—the player opposing the server (p. 99)

RECTUS FOOT—a "normal" arched foot (p. 96)

RETURN OF SERVE—the act of returning a ball to the opponent's court following his/her serve (p. 54)

SERVE—stroke which begins play in a point or game (p. 35)

SERVE AND VOLLEY GAME—strategy in singles play in which player approaches the net immediately after serving the ball (p. 84)

SERVER—the player who first delivers the ball in a game (p. 99)

SERVICE LINE—the boundary line at the back of the service court (p. 100)

SET—player who first wins six games and who wins by at least a margin of two games (p. 106)

SIDELINE—the line which runs from the net to the baseline and marks the outer edge of the playing court (p. 100)

SLICE—rotation on a ball in reverse of the topspin; also known as a backspin rotation on the ball (p. 53)

SPLIT-STEP–a slight jump landing on the balls of the feet when advancing toward the net (p. 85)

STATIC STRETCH–a slow stretching exercise through a range of motion with a hold position at the end (p. 15)

STRATEGY–a plan of attack for placing your opponent in a position of disadvantage (p. 83)

STRENGTH–the force a muscle exerts against a resistance in one maximal effort (p. 5)

SWEET SPOT–see CENTER OF PERCUSSION

TIE-BREAK GAME–in operation when the score reaches six games all in any set (p. 107)

TOPSPIN–an exaggerated overspin (p. 54)

TWO BACK–strategy in doubles play where both partners play the baseline position (p. 87)

TWO-HANDED BACKHAND–an alternate backhand stroke in which two hands are placed together on the racquet (p. 28)

TWO UP–strategy in doubles play where both partners play the net position (p. 85)

USLTA–United States Lawn Tennis Association, later to become the USTA (p. 2)

USTA–United States Tennis Association, the governing body for tennis in the United States (p. 2)

VOLLEY–a stroke, other than the serve, in which the ball is hit before it touches the ground (p. 40)

WIGHTMAN CUP–annual competition between womens' teams from the United States and England (p. 2)

WIMBLEDON CHAMPIONSHIPS–considered to be the most prestigious of the four major tennis tournaments; held annually in England (p. 2)

WIND-UP PHASE–phase of a serve characterized by a wide circular motion of the arms in preparation for ball contact (p. 37)

UNITED STATES
TENNIS ASSOCIATION (USTA)

70 West Red Oak Lane
White Plains, New York 10604-3602
(914) 696-7000

The USTA is the national governing body for tennis in the United States and is a member of the International Tennis Federation. Its purposes are to:

1. promote the development of tennis as a means of healthful recreation and fitness;
2. establish and maintain rules of play and high standards of amateurism and good sportsmanship;
3. foster national and international amateur tennis tournaments;
4. encourage, sanction, and conduct tennis tournaments and competitions;
5. assist with the development of health, character and responsible citizenship.

USTA SECTIONAL NAMES AND ADDRESSES

Caribbean Tennis Association
P.O. Box 40439
Minillas Station
Saturce, PR 00940

Eastern Tennis Association
550 Mam Roneck Ave. #505
Harrison, NY 10528

Florida Tennis Association
1280 S.W. 36th Ave. Suite #305
Pompano Beach, FL 33069-4868

Hawaii Pacific Tennis Association
2615 S. King St. #2A
Honolulu, HI 96826

Intermountain Tennis Association
1201 S. Parker Rd. #200
Denver, CO 80231

Mid-Atlantic Tennis Association
2230George C. Marshall Dr. #E
Falls Church, VA 22043

USTA/Middle States
700 S. Henderson Rd. #210
King of Prussia, PA 19406

Missouri Valley Tennis Association
722 Walnut, Suite #1
Kansas City, MO 64106

USTA New England
Box 587
Needham, MA 02194

Northern California Tennis Assoc.
1350 Loop Rd., Suite #200
Alameda, CA 94502-7081

Northwestern Tennis Association
5525 Cedar Lake Rd.
St. Louis Park, MN 55416

USTA/Pacific Northwest
4840 S.W. Western Ave.
Beaverton, OR 97005-3430

Southern California Tennis Assoc.
P.O. Box 240015
Los Angeles, CA 90024-9115

Southern Tennis Association
200 Sandy Springs Place, #200
Atlanta, GA 30328

USTA Southwest Section
6330-2 E. Thomas Rd., Suite #120
Scottsdale, AZ 85251-7056

Texas Tennis Association
2111 Dickson, Suite #33
Austin, TX 78704

Western Tennis Association
8720 Castle Creek Pkwy.,
Suite #329
Indianapolis, IN 46250

SAMPLE TENNIS EXAM

Multiple Choice

1. In 1873, the modern day game of tennis was introduced in the country of:
   a. France
   b. Britain
   c. Australia
   d. United States

2. The "Grand Slam" of tennis tournaments includes:
   a. French Open, Australian Open, U. S. Open, Wimbledon
   b. Wimbledon, U. S. Open, French Open, European Open
   c. British Open, U.S. Open, French Open, Canadian Open
   d. French Open, British Open, U. S. Open, Australian Open

3. Team competition involving men from different countries is called:
   a. World Championships
   b. Ryder Cup
   c. International Championships
   d. Davis Cup

4. General guidelines for lifting weights include all but one of the following:
   a. alternate opposing muscle groups
   b. continue breathing throughout the exercise
   c. move the weights through a full range of motion
   d. use explosive movements when exercising eccentrically

5. General guidelines for stretching include all but one of the following:
   a. begin the stretching program by light jogging or a brisk walk
   b stretch only those muscle groups which will be used in playing
   c. continue breathing throughout the exercise
   d. stretch before and after playing

6. All but one of the following activities provide good aerobic

conditioning:
- a.   racquetball
- b.   swimming
- c.   jogging
- d.   cycling

7. All but one of the following is desirable in an aerobic conditioning program:
- a.   should be done 3-5 days per week
- b.   should be 30-40 minutes in duration
- c.   should be done at 60%-80% of maximum heart rate
- d.   should be done seasonally

8. The most important phase in either the forehand or backhand drive is:
- a.   the ready position
- b.   initial reaction
- d.   follow-through

9. The contact phase execution includes all but one of the following:
- a.   rotation initiated by the shoulders
- b.   racquet at hip or waist level parallel to ground
- c.   racquet strings facing direction of intended hit
- d.   free hand working with racquet hand

10. The follow-through is important because:
- a.   it helps to prevent injury
- b.   it serves as a feedback mechanism
- c.   it aids in maintenance of racquet speed through contact
- d.   all of the above
- e.   a and b only

11. The contact phase for the one-handed backhand drive includes all but one of the following:
- a.   racquet arm pulls from the shoulder
- b.   free hand works with racquet hand
- c.   racquet at hip level parallel to ground
- d.   ball contact even with front foot and racquet length away from body

12. The wind-up phase during the serve includes all but one of the following:
- a.   hands drop simultaneously as weight is shifted through

toss
b.   hands separate as front knee is approached
c.   "T" position of arms at ball release
d.   ball toss height equal to height of racquet extension

13. During the contact phase for the serve, all but one of the following occurs:
a.   weight forward
b.   racquet strings facing target area
c.   head stationary and looking at ball
d.   hit down on the ball

14. All but one of the following is desirable during the contact phase of the volley:
a.   opposite foot and both hands react toward ball simultaneously
b.   shortened backswing
c.   body angled 45 degrees to net
d.   eyes on ball throughout

15. During the initial reaction phase in the overhead, all but one of the following occurs:
a.   step and turn, weight forward
b.   hands above head
c.   elbow bent to backscratch position
d.   racquet side foot 3 feet behind and left of contact point

16. The drop shot preparation includes all but one of the following:
a.   step and turn
b.   short or no backswing
c.   weight forward
d.   hands working as one unit

17. The most aggressive type of singles strategy is:
a.   a baseline game
b.   an all-court game
c.   a serve and volley game

18. The most aggressive type of doubles strategy is:
a.   one up, one back
b.   two up
c.   two back

19. The place on the racquet strings where the least vibration is felt when the ball hits is known as:
a.   center of gravity
b.   center of mass

    c.   center of vibration
    d.   center of percussion

20.   Which of the following features is desirable in selecting a tennis shoe?
    a.   traction
    b.   stability in the forefoot and rearfoot
    c.   cushioning
    d.   flexibility
    e.   toe box reinforcement
    f.   all of the above

21.   The player winning the toss may choose or require his opponent to choose:
    a.   the right to be server or receiver
    b.   the side
    c.   the right to be server and the side
    d.   a and b
    e.   all of the above

22.   All of the following are faults during the serve except for one:
    a.   server misses the ball in attempting to serve it
    b.   ball does not land in proper service court
    c.   ball touches permanent fixture other than the net, strap, or band before it touches the ground.
    d.   server serves the ball with an underhand motion before it hits the ground

23.   A player may lose a point in all of the following situations except one:
    a.   ball in play touches the racquet more than once
    b.   follow-through is over the net after properly returning the ball
    c.   ball in play touches any part of the body
    d.   ball in play lands outside any boundary line on opponent's court

24.   All of the following are the unwritten rules of tennis etiquette except for one:
    a.   Be sure your opponent is ready to receive serve.
    b.   Announce game score prior to serving each point.
    c.   If in doubt as to whether ball was "in" or "out", replay the point.
    d.   Acknowledge a good play by your opponent.

True or False

25.   It is speculated that the first game of tennis was played over 5000 years ago in China.

26. The early game of tennis was played on grass surfaces.

27. Team competition involving women from different   countries is known as the Wightman Cup.

28. Physical fitness is one of the benefits of playing tennis.

29. An all-around conditioning program involves strength, flexibility, and cardiovascular endurance.

30. Strength is defined as how much work can be performed per unit of time.

31. Power can be developed by lifting lighter weights for more repetitions rather than lifting heavier weights for fewer repetitions.

32. Stretching prior to playing tennis may prevent muscle soreness afterwards.

33. The game of tennis is considered to be an aerobic activity.

34. The two basic groundstrokes in tennis are the forehand and the backhand.

35. The initial reaction to an oncoming ball is a step with the rear foot parallel to the baseline, and a turn.

36. A right-handed player initially steps with the right foot when setting up a backhand.

37. The two-handed backhand limits the range of movement permitted by the player.

38. The major difference between the forehand and one-handed backhand drives during the contact phase is a lack of body rotation in the backhand.

39. The back hand of the two-handed backhand functions in a similar manner to the forehand drive.

40. A critical part of the approach/half volley shot is the ability to hold the ball on the strings.

41. The movement pattern of a serve is similar to that of a throwing motion.

42. The Continental grip is recommended for the volley stroke.

43.   The lob can be used as an offensive stroke to allow more time in preparing for the next shot.

44.   A critical part of the approach/half volley shot is a   shortened backswing with a complete follow-through.

45.   Grass courts favor the serve and volley type player because of the way the ball bounces.

46.   Generally speaking, the tighter the string tension, the less control you have over the racquet.

47.   Extra duty nap on a tennis ball is desirable for hard court surfaces.

48.   Generally speaking, a person with a high-arched foot would benefit from a shoe with a flexible arch support.

49.   A straight-lasted shoe would benefit a person with a flat-arched foot because it has more arch support.

50.   There is no limit to the number of let balls that may be made on a service.

51.   Players change sides after each person has served a game, and then alternately after every two games.

52.   In doubles, the order of receiving may not be changed during a set, but may be changed at the beginning a new set.

53.   The score is called deuce if both players have won three points.

54.   Player A wins 6 games, Player B wins 5 games. Player A is declared winner of the set.

55.   In a singles tie-break game, a winner is declared when one player reaches 7 points and leads by a margin of 2 points.

ANSWERS

Multiple Choice		True-False	
1.	B	25.	T
2.	A	26.	T
3.	D	27.	F
4.	D	28.	T
5.	B	29.	T
6.	A	30.	F
7.	D	31.	T
8.	B	32.	T
9.	A	33.	F
10.	D	34.	T
11.	B	35.	T
12.	C	36.	F
13.	D	37.	T
14.	B	38.	T
15.	A	39.	T
16.	C	40.	F
17.	C	41.	T
18.	B	42.	T
19.	D	43.	F
20.	F	44.	T
21.	D	45.	T
22.	D	46.	F
23.	B	47.	T
24.	C	48.	T
		49.	T
		50.	T
		51.	F
		52.	T
		53.	T
		54.	F
		55.	T

LIBRARY
ST. LOUIS COMMUNITY COLLEGE
AT FLORISSANT VALLEY